Myths, Management & Mastery of Vacation Rentals

by
Jeramie L. Worley
With contributions by
Richard Carraway CPA, Brad Moncado & Kelly Worley

A note to reader:

This publication is designed to provide accurate and authoritative information in regard to the subject matter covered. It is sold with the understanding that the author and publisher are not engaged in rendering legal, accounting or other professional service. This publication is for entertainment purposes only. If legal or expert assistance is required, the services of a competent professional person should be sought.

Worley & Associates 225 Corporate Place, Suite P-1 Branson, MO 65616
Worleyandassociatesinfo@gmail.com

DEDICATED to my wife who came with me on this adventurous career. Thank you, Kelly, for your enduring love and compassion, helpfulness and belief. I also dedicate this book to my real estate team who have taken on the burden of holding down the fort until I can get the job of writing a book done. To all of my clients and friends who have joined me in the buying, operating and selling of vacation rentals, you are phenomenal people. You are smart, passionate entrepreneurs, and I'm thankful to be able to do business with you. Also, to my parents who donated heaps of sweat equity on my first few vacation rental remodels, and to my grandparents, Ed and Barb Kendrick, who made an investment in me that I will never be able to repay.

CONTENTS

I want to thank Jeramie, Brad and Richard for giving me an opportunity to write the foreword for their book. I'm always inspired when I see people reach a helping hand down to those in need and aiding them in climbing the ladder of success. Since these fellas are students of mine, I'm even more proud of them for it.

When I first got involved with real estate, I was a dead broke auto mechanic trying to make enough money to make ends meet. Within two years, I'd amassed 276 units and was a millionaire on paper, but still, I had lessons to learn. The School of Hard Knocks taught me that my lower income properties or "war zone" properties, as I like to call them, were sucking me dry financially and mentally. My days were spent solving their petty problems and listening to all the worthless excuses of why they couldn't pay rent.

You won't find any "war zones" in the vacation rental real estate markets. These properties are full of people who are on vacation, they are happy to be there, they don't stay long enough to do a whole lot of damage to a property, and the best part…they pay up front.

If you know anything about me, you know I like a Golden Goose! This is a property that lays golden eggs every month, and the longer you keep it, the more money you make. In my Pretty House System, which you can find on my website at www.ronlegrand.com, we show you how you can make big money in beautiful houses without ever having to flip or remodel them.

What I like about Jeramie's book, is that you can combine what I teach in my Pretty House System with what you'll learn in his book to find golden geese that lay gigantic golden eggs.

The Vacation Rental Real Estate market is booming, and this book isn't just a stack of good information, it's a system for analyzing, managing and collecting bigger returns through beautiful properties in areas where there is a steady flow of tourist traffic.

Jeramie started out a lot like me, a broke guy with the idea that there has got to be a better way. After nearly a decade of buying, managing and selling vacation rentals and earning overwhelming returns even through the worst real estate market in history, he's learned a few things that are worth reading about. Above all, he loves to share. He's teamed up with some great thinkers and great talent to give you a real practical plan to get better returns.

Let this book inspire you to take action. You can't lean on a shovel and expect that hole to dig itself! You've got to take this information and put it to good use. If you are even slightly considering nightly rentals as an option, then this is the book that will get you started on the path to making money.

I'd love it if you did so you can tell me all about your success at one of my live events!

Ron LeGrand

Chapter One
Baring It All

I ran head-first into the vacation rental business out of the outright desperate need to change the financial quality of my life. I started with no money and no equity, and within five years, I was the leading expert in vacation rentals in the Branson, Missouri real estate market. I struggled up a mountain of knowledge while operating the business. I did everything from changing light bulbs on rickety forty-foot ladders, cleaning Bisquick off of bed sheets and hand delivering toilet paper. So, I worked my way first-hand to finally closing on $600,000 vacation homes. I was determined to please. I kept going because I figured out one important thing. Whether you are extremely wealthy or want to be, we all need the same thing: a better rate of return on our time.

Perhaps you are looking to the nightly rental business to provide a high-paying, part-time job that you can do in your spare time or a high-yield enterprise where you are putting those nights to work for you. Either way, you'll find it to be a rewarding endeavor. This book will keep you from having to do some of the questionable things I did to get to a level of success. I'm not going to sugar-coat my experience; I want you to really know what it means to dive in.

In 2008, the real estate market had hit a critical low. Things were bleak. I was a full-time real estate agent in a second-home market and had only closed four deals that year. I had written and negotiated more contracts that year than any other year, but people were fidgety. Most home buyers were walking around town with a red pen, slashing prices, and sellers were shocked at the horribly low offers. It was so bad, I considered changing the name of my company to "Jeramie's Low-Ball Realty." In addition, buyers wouldn't pay the sellers' bottom line price or they freaked out from watching too much Fox News and walked away all together. With the economy in shambles, I had a product that nobody wanted: second homes. Since second homes are a luxury item, my business was about to pay the ultimate price. I had no money in the bank. My wife was pregnant with our second child and had just been laid off from her job. I also had taken on a part-time job to help with the piling bills, and in a twist of bad luck, I had gotten notice that I had just been laid off from my second job, as well. I could hear the wolves scratching at the door.

Accompanied by a feeling of numbness, I went to my real estate office every day. I was too downtrodden to nurture my ambition. Simply put, I just went in. I'm not sure if I was in shock, denial or just operating on autopilot, but I went through the motions each day of being a real estate agent. I kept lead generating for buyers and sellers, researching good deals and picking up the phone to sell them. Nothing was working. I came home each night empty-handed, and my beautiful, amazing, smart, but hormonal wife would look at me and ask, "Why are you still doing this?" I couldn't answer the question. Real estate was the only type of investment that I had a real knack for. It was the only thing I'd ever made any money at. I had instincts and passion for building wealth through owning real property. It seemed wrong to quit, but my back was to the wall, and I had gotten to the point where I had no choice. I'd read tons of books for Heaven's sake! How on earth could I be smart and broke at the same time? I remember thinking that if I had the horrible morals to become a prostitute, or at the very least, a timeshare salesman, I could attempt to provide for my family. So, how could I sell all of these second homes without violating all of my values?

I racked my brain until it finally landed on planet Nightly Rental. I'd heard of them but didn't really understand how powerful they could be. I lived in a vacation destination, but I was not taking advantage of all of the opportunities that existed there. Determined, I went to work, learning everything I could about nightly rentals, and it didn't take long before I found the property that would change my life forever.

It was an amazing deal. It was a fully-furnished vacation home in a vacation rental community. It was a builder closeout, new to the market and mine for the taking. I didn't have any money, though. I couldn't qualify for a loan. I had an amazing opportunity, and as usual, I had horrible timing. It was like finding a vacuum cleaner at the store that you know costs $500, but there it is, on sale for $35 bucks. It was just too good to pass on. So, I took my two cents and some talent, grabbed the phone, and started calling everyone I knew. Call after call, it seemed that people either had no interest or understanding of vacation rentals or, due to the economy, they just were not willing to take on any risk whatsoever. I was desperate to find a buyer for this opportunity.

I'd been trying to convince everyone I knew that this was a deal. I was desperate enough to talk to my family about it, and they have a risk tolerance so low they wouldn't even buy a different brand of toilet paper. Imagine my shock when, in a conversation over dinner, my extremely conservative grandpa who had been out of debt for decades, said "yes" and decided to go for it.

Grandpa said yes to my wild idea. He had been hesitant to get into a new investment, but he was looking for a tax shelter and a place for a $20,000 CD that had just come due. He was about to put the investment in municipal bonds when I told him about the property. I agreed to manage the property for him and send him a check each month for the profit. He agreed, we closed on the sale and we began our adventure together. Soon after that sale, the developer of the vacation rental community, in which Grandpa had bought his vacation home, approached me to apply for the opportunity to become the listing agent for the entire development. Either I'd put the screws to them pretty good representing Grandpa or perhaps they were just ready for a change. Nevertheless, just a few weeks before my son was born that year, I was awarded the position of Sales Manager and Listing Agent for the development. My journey to becoming the premier vacation rental specialist in Branson, Missouri had had just begun.

I had the opportunity to sell vacation rental homes in the worst real estate market in history and help my clients earn very high rates of return during a time that other investments were tarnishing. Since I had first-hand knowledge of operating and marketing a vacation rental, I was uniquely equipped to help newcomers understand the business before they bought. Then, as an added value, I would stay on to coach them to success after the sale. In addition to all of this, my wife started a cleaning business for vacation rentals as a way to bring in extra money to our budget after baby number two was born. Within two years, she was cleaning over forty nightly rentals and had a staff of eight employees. Because of her experience cleaning the homes, we were able to witness the successful booking strategies and success levels of all types of vacation rentals from one bedroom to seven bedrooms, single family homes versus condo, lakefront versus non-lakefront properties and peak season versus off-peak. Together, we built a mass of knowledge and experience that solidified us as the "go to" people for advice and information on nightly rentals.

We gave away this knowledge for years just to help see people succeed when they took their first step in this new type of investment. The act of writing a book on the subject is more of a function of finally jotting down the advice once and for all. You can build a great empire, but most people start out like I did, by keeping your day job and getting one property. Think of it as a high-paying, part-time night job. It's fun to accept a booking request while you are holding your smart phone in bed at night. Cha ching! You've got money! You just got paid by a stranger, and you didn't do anything you couldn't tell your grandmother about.

I want this book to serve you and help you find and operate a successful business in nightly rental real estate. I want you to see the power in renting out nights instead of whole years. Let this strategy work for you, rather than you simply exchanging time for money by getting up each day exhausted, working for someone who probably doesn't care about you at all. I hope your family draws closer, not just in using and enjoying your vacation home, but through building wealth and operating a small business together. I pray your home is able to bless other families and that through your home, memories are made and lives are mended. The information you are about to read in this book is not just my experience. I'm going to introduce you to some sharp people. Our teaching comes from first-hand, on-the-ground, collective experience and wisdom. It is compiled from successful professionals who are immersed in every aspect of the business from real estate deals, property owners, cleaners, marketing companies, CPA's and even vacation rental travelers. This book is for the three types of people: first-time vacation rental buyers, seasoned owners who need some additional coaching and real estate investors who have never witnessed the power of vacation rental cash flow. This is the manual I wish I had when I'd gotten started.

Chapter Two

Exploding the Vacation Rental Myths

Most people are too smart for their own good. I may be guilty of this. I can latch onto an opinion that doesn't serve me, but I will argue that point until I'm blue in the face. Here is an example: I thought that money was hard to make. I thought it takes money to make money. I believed that money was scarce. I must have been washing with money-repellent soap. I had all of this knowledge on how to operate a nightly rental, but I didn't own one. I was selling them and managing them and gaining a ton of experience, but I was ready to start owning one. I was a salesman, a property manager and, at times, a maid. When would a nightly rental show up on my balance sheet? I didn't have a down payment; I wasn't flush with cash. Yet, in my disgruntled, frustrated days, believing these lies about my current situation, it took an innocent child to completely change my mindset.

A few years ago, I was driving my daughter to kindergarten, and she exploded my view of money in one sentence. She was getting used to the new rules of her classroom, and the teacher had set up a point system. If you were disciplined, you'd lose a point, and it was a very effective tactic. My daughter was disappointed on the way to school one day, so I asked her about it. "Daddy," she said, "I lost a point yesterday."
"What did you do to lose the point?" I asked.
"I was talking during class," she admitted.
She was very upset. She hated losing the point. Seeing this as the perfect opportunity teach my little girl about

following the rules of life, I attempted to apply the principle using a real-life example.

"That's right, honey," I started in, "if I don't follow the rules, I get consequences, too. For example, if I drive this car too fast on the way to school, the police will pull me over and give me a ticket."

"What happens if you get a ticket?"

In the spirit of honesty, I replied, "If Daddy gets a ticket, he will have to pay money to a lawyer and get if fixed. It will cost a lot of money. Daddy doesn't have a lot of--"

"YOU DON'T UNDERSTAND!" she interrupted. Money is not rare. You can always go and make more money. When I lose a point, I can never get it back. Ever."

Her point was made, clearly and with logic. I was both proud and humbled by her perfect little mind. Money is not rare…her words burned into my brain. It is a renewable resource, and it is available today, right now, everywhere. When I spend it, it's not gone forever. I can go make more. I thought of all of the oceans of money that are moved around in the markets. I thought of all the money that is wasted by governments, universities and huge corporations. All I needed was a tiny bit of it. With it, I could put it to work for me at incredible rates of return. Money will always follow a good idea, and I had tons of them. So, I hugged my daughter and dropped her off at school. From that day on, I charged forward down this path because I believed then that my greatest resource was my *resourcefulness*. It was then that I decided to negotiate my way into an equity position in a high cash-flow property with zero money down. That decision changed everything because after I did it, I was able to help others use the same strategy.

I don't need to convince you that real estate is an effective wealth-building tool. There have been many great minds that have come before me to convince you of this, from Gary Keller and his book, "The Millionaire Real Estate Investor" to Robert Kiyosaki's "Rich Dad Poor Dad." My goal is not to convince you to buy real estate, but rather, if you are going to buy real estate, buy a nightly rental because you can tap into a rich reservoir of cash flow that very few other property types offer. For example, in some markets, a seven-bedroom vacation rental can outperform a twelve-unit apartment building, and I'll show you how in a later chapter. I would like to focus this chapter on the myths and reasons most people don't even consider vacation rental investments and the realities that debunk them.

I lead regular seminars for real estate investors, and at the beginning of the workshop I love to ask two questions. The first question is, "How many of you own or have ever owned a vacation rental?" When I ask this question, about one percent of the group raises their hands. Then I ask, "How many of you are planning to go or have ever gone on vacation?" When I ask this question, about ninety-nine percent of the group raises their hands. At this point, the group understands the power of vacation rental real estate because they are already using it, and more than likely, multiple times per year.

Another question I ask in these workshops is, "What are your current perceptions of vacation rentals?" Sometimes I use the term "nightly rentals" or "short-term rentals" because there are many areas of the country, such as college towns, sporting events, or medical miles,

17

that are not vacation destinations but offer promising opportunities for a property owner. This is where I find out why more people are not pulling the trigger, and here are a few of the myths:

MYTH # 1
YOU CANNOT MAKE IT IN VACATION RENTALS BECAUSE OF THE OFF SEASON

The "off season" is the time of the year in a specific vacation destination when, seasonally, vacation traffic is light or nonexistent. How on earth can an investor make it when three to four months of the year are off the table? It is a valid question, but the better question to ask is, "What if I made so much money in the peak season that it didn't matter if I earned a dime in the off season?" Here is a real life scenario for you.

Long-Term Rental

The values in the the following scenarios will vary in different markets, but the opportunity for finding a vacation rental that reaps real returns exists by discovering those markets where purchase prices are still reasonable and saturation has not occurred. For example, in my real estate market in Branson, Missouri, the market value to rent a five-bedroom, three-bath home on a long-term basis is about $1,700 per month for an average property. This is assuming that you are fortunate, you have zero vacancy and you can rent it for all twelve months. The most you can earn that year is $20,400 ($1,700 x 12 = $20,400). This is your Gross Operating Income. It is the most money you can earn from this property in one year, and you have to subtract all of your expenses from this each year.

Nightly Rental

Assuming we are in the same market, the per-night value to rent a five-bedroom, three-bath nightly rental home can range from $300 - $550 per night. Assuming conservatively, let's say that we rent it out for $325 per night. Let's assume the off season is about two-and-a-half months long, but you won't book every night every month, so let's use a fifty-five percent vacancy rate and say we can only rent it out for 164 nights. The rest of the year we'll say it sits vacant. 164 x $325 per night = $53,300 per year. Taxes and cleaning fees are charged above and beyond the nightly rent amount, so we do not need to subtract those expenses. $53,300 is your Gross Operating Income, and the important thing to note here is that this is not even the most you can earn because this is only 164 nights out of the year.

Long-Term Rental

5-Bedroom 3-Bath Home
$1700 per month

Max nights 365 per year
Vacancy Rate 0% (365 Nights Rented)

Total Annual Rent **$20,400**
Additional amount you can earn that year $0

Nightly Rental

5-Bedroom 3-Bath Home
$325 per night

Max nights 365 per year
Vacancy Rate 55% (164 Nights Rented)

Total Annual Rent **$53,300**
Additional amount you can earn that year _____ x 201 nights

We have not even gotten to the best part. When you choose to invest in a vacation rental, you get your money up front. Your agreement may change based on your market, but upon taking a reservation, we always take a deposit of half-payment down when the booking is made; the remaining half is paid anywhere from 30-60 days before guests arrive. By the time the guest has arrived, you have already gotten your money up front. They don't even get the door code to the property until all monies have been received. This is a stark opposition to long-term rentals where you have to wait for your money each month and hope like heck you get it on time. With vacation rentals, you've diversified the property over many families over the course of the year, and you depend on them to help you pay your mortgage and expenses. Yet in a long-term rental scenario, you are typically relying on one family to pay the mortgage and expenses. It seems to me that in a long-term rental scenario, you are really putting all of your eggs in one basket. This, combined with a lower earnings potential, seems like a much higher risk scenario. I'd take an off season over a bad long-term renter, no question.

MYTH # 2
PEOPLE WILL TRASH MY HOME

In a long-term rental scenario, it is best to check people out before you give them possession of your home. You take an application, run a credit check, call a few references and take a security and damage deposit before you give them keys. I always looked on the credit report to make sure that the people I was renting the home to didn't know the court system better than I did. These are good layers of protection, but they do not protect you from your renter's deep desire to operate a tattoo parlor out of the living room or from their recently paroled friends. Back in the days before I got hooked on nightly rentals, I went to collect monthly rent from two college girls we had rented to who were about a week late paying. They had stopped returning our calls, so I dropped by to knock on the door and see how things were going. I could hear people inside, but no one came to the door. I continued to knock louder until an unfriendly dude came out with a baseball bat in one hand a steaming hot cup of nothing in the other. I took the hint! Instead of going home with my money, I went home with a strong desire to take karate lessons and a desperate need for some clean shorts. I also got the benefit of knowing I was about to get a comprehensive education on learning how to evict someone. They trashed my home. I cleaned it up while frantically searching for a good renter. I even offered a great discount on the monthly rent in the hopes to take my pick of the crop of good renters. This time, I rented it to a quiet-mannered, single gal with a small dog. She stayed for two years and after a while got behind on her rent. We gave her some grace and helped her get caught up, but eventually it was the same story. We gave her thirty-days' notice that her month-to-month lease term was up, and she stopped returning our calls. With no income from that property and no contact from the renter, we ended up having to evict her also. When we finally regained possession of the property, her small dog had laid waste (literally) to every inch of the place. There would have been less poop in the east wing of a diarrhea ward. I wish I was exaggerating. Her pet trashed our property.

The response to this myth is that, yes, people and their friends and pets might trash your property because they have time to access and live in your property. The more time you give them to live in and access the property, the more opportunity they have to trash it. Human beings are filthy creatures, and given the opportunity and the time, we will destroy anything. This is why a long-term rental is a much less favorable scenario because, in addition to maxing out with a lower gross operating income, people are in your home 365 days a year. You hope!

Now, consider a vacation rental where there are only people in your home half of the year, and then it's only for 3-5 days at a time. What is even better? During that time, they are not even in your home very much. They are out at the beach, theme park, restaurant or show. They are really only in your home a short time, and half of that time they are sleeping. Say what you want about people trashing your home, but I'll stick with vacation rentals.

MYTH # 3
I CAN'T MANAGE A VACATION HOME IN FLORDIA ALL THE WAY FROM KANSAS!

One of the reasons many people shy away from owning a vacation rental is the perceived notion that you have to be onsite for anything that might happen. That might have been the case at one time, but the internet and the information age have transformed everything. Not only can you advertise your property online, you can take bookings over email, process credit card payments online and you can also receive notifications from the lock on your door that your renters have arrived and that they've moved the thermostat up by five degrees. Most of the time, you can do all of this from your smart phone wherever you are, even while you are on vacation! We coach our clients to build a power team of good cleaners and responsive handymen in the event that someone would need to go by the property. Your cleaning staff are your eyes and ears and are probably your most important partner. In later chapters, we will get into how to select a cleaning team and what questions you should ask before you hire them.

You can hire a property manager, and this will alleviate much of your concern, but it can also alleviate much of your profit. A good property manager can be an asset, and if you want to use one, you will have to work a little harder to find a better deal when you buy so you can still get some good cash flow.

Simply put, most of my clients own and manage more than one vacation rental, and very few of them live in the same town that the property is in. If we backwoods slow-talking Midwesterners can do it, then surely the rest of y'all can, as well.

Here is a final note on managing your property yourself. You will get calls. If you are in the real estate business, your renters will call you. They are paying your mortgage, so for Heaven's sake, pick up the phone! However, when you own a vacation rental, many times the calls are different. Sure, they may have trouble with a door code or maybe operating the TV inputs, but more often than not, we get a call from our renters when they get to the property to tell us how beautiful the home is. They are thankful and happy, and that is a rewarding feeling. I can say with one-hundred-percent certainty that I've never gotten this type of call with a long-term rental.

MYTH # 4
VACATION RENTALS ARE MORE OF A RISK...
ESPECIALLY IN A BAD ECONOMY!

Many things are more of a risk in a bad economy. All of the extras go out the window, like candy bars, clothes and certainly extravagant vacations. During these times, people don't want to stop vacationing; they just want to vacation smarter and maybe closer to home. Families will band together and pool their resources to find a bigger property that will accommodate all of them. The benefit to them is that they can spread out the nightly rate over three to four families. $350 per night divided by 3 families is only $116 per night, and when you consider you would be getting a 2,500 square-foot home with private bedrooms, screened-in decks, great views, two

living rooms, some amenities and a full kitchen so you
don't have to go out for every meal, the value and savings
start to add up. Frankly, I don't know why anyone would
ever stay in a hotel ever again. Why would you want to
live in a 200 square-foot room with a coffee pot in the
bathroom and a view of the parking lot? During the
years between 2008 and 2011 when the real estate market
was in recession, the vacation rental industry broke out to
become one of the fastest-growing trends in travel.

In my experience as a real estate broker, I've found
that the income that vacation rental properties earn
during poor economic time actually prevents short sales
and foreclosures. If these distressed sales are eliminated
from a neighborhood altogether, then that helps keep
values higher for everyone. I can say with conviction
that one-hundred-percent of my clients who purchased a
vacation rental during the time frame from 2008–2011 is
in a better equity position today.

There are more positive factors driving second-home
and vacation rental markets now than ever before, and
it would be risky to not pay attention to them. Per the
last United States Census in 2010, the population of the
country was 308,745,538; on July 4, 2013, according to
http://www.census.gov/popclock/ it was reported to be
316,148,990. I love to go to this website because you can
literally see the population of the United States and the
world growing right in front of your eyes.

Harry Dent is a Harvard educated business strategist
and author, as well as a leading expert in long-term
demographic research. In one of his diagrams titled "The
Real Estate Life Cycle," he dictates that people between
the ages of 48–68 are buying second homes and vacation
homes. So when you think about it, over 23 million

people are looking for pre-retirement homes and vacation homes right now. Many of my clients are shopping for a retirement home that they can use and enjoy today and use the rental income to pay if off by the time they are ready to retire. They can rent out the home to earn income or at least subsidize the payment until they are ready to sell their primary home and retire. Either way, they are able to use and enjoy the property while they are in good health to do so. Vacation rentals, in my experience, are no more of a risk in a bad economy than anything else, particularly those vacation destinations which are largely driving destinations. Even when gas prices here high, families still choose to jump in the car for a three-hour trip over a $2,000 plane ticket.

Remember, when times get hard, people don't stop going on vacation, they just vacation smarter. More and more people are starting to realize that vacation rentals are a smarter and more comfortable choice. In fact, once I started focusing on selling vacation homes, I found that more people were moving money out of the stock market because they were tired of devastating losses and lack of control of their investments. They wanted to get out of the fear and greed business and into the vacation rental business.

Chapter Three
What to Buy, When to Buy & How to Buy

The experience of buying a vacation rental is one of the most rewarding things you can do. It immediately puts your mind in vacation mode. You begin to experience what it might be like to be a guest in the homes you are looking at, and don't forget, you may be buying this to use and enjoy for yourself. I've found that buyers, especially investors, are more positively charged when shopping for this type of property than a flip or a remodel. Your primary residence is a fun purchase, yet typically most buyers put too much pressure on themselves to find the perfect home. I understand completely. You will spend the next five to seven years, maybe more, in this one home. If your eyes are bigger than your stomach and you've been in homes a bit more than you can afford, then you have to start going down the list of things you'll have to do without. It can be bittersweet; I've seen it so many times as a real estate agent.

A purchase made solely for investment can get cold and boring after you've done it a few times. All you do is look at sticks and bricks and numbers. You may look at a trashy piece of property and muster the capital or sweat equity to bring it back to its neighborhood glory. In this type of purchase, the exciting sensation comes with seeing the opportunity that others cannot see. The thrill for flippers or holders is in winning some equity.

Buying a vacation home that you will also use for nightly rental, on the contrary, gives you the best of both worlds. The pressure is off to find the perfect place because you only need to find a place for you and your guests to unplug for a while. You are free to make decisions from a place of calculated risk and positive drive. After all, this is a place where people will be spending time off. You and your creativity, thoughts and ideas will enhance their experience and bring them closer to reducing stress and worry (depending on which family members they bring along). You can still win equity, but you can also win furniture and bookings and get a big fat check at closing for all of those prepaid bookings. That is a rewarding thought and should exhilarate the newcomer and seasoned investor alike.

Here is a fun example. After two years, Grandpa and I decided to sell the first vacation rental and upgrade it from a four-bedroom to a five-bedroom. It made sense because if I was going to spend the time booking the property, I'd rather book a five-bedroom than a four-bedroom. I would be literally taking the same number of phone calls and emails, but with a five-bedroom I could earn an extra $100 per night. This is when I first realized that he had not bought a piece of real estate. He had bought a money machine, and the question was: how much money did we want it to spit out? It took some courage for Grandpa to buy the first vacation rental, but after two years of success, he was emboldened to invest a bit more capital to buy a bigger money machine. This is how it is with most people buying a nightly rental. You have to balance your level of risk tolerance with your desired rate of return. In other words, there is going to be risk in any investment you make, but the best part about real estate, especially vacation rentals, is that you can analyze your first-year rate of return before you buy based on the formula I am going to give you. In this chapter, we will give you some tools to help you analyze the investment. We also want to make sure that you have done some careful homework before you put on your game face and start slinging offers.

THE FIVE STEPS TO BUYING
A VACATION RENTAL

Step #1 Get crystal clear about the intended use of the property

Before you even start looking, you'll need to know how you are going to use the property. One of the first vacation rentals I ever sold was to woman who has become a good friend and mentor to me. I've helped her buy and sell over a dozen vacation rentals, but I'll never forget the first one. When she called me on one of my listings, she was looking for something very specific.

She said, "Last year I was trying to plan a vacation for my family, and I couldn't find anything. Everything was booked! I don't want that to happen anymore. I want to find a vacation home for my family to use, and I want to rent it out when we are not using it!"

That was a clear business plan, and as a real estate agent, I had two objectives: I had to find a place that she felt at home and, at the same time, a place where nightly rental was permitted. She didn't confuse her plan with the thought of retirement or the with buying a lot that she may someday build on. (Which, by the way, many people never get around to doing.) She had a clear idea of what she was ready to buy, today. She was pre-qualified and knew exactly what her budget was. Fast-forward to present day. She now owns over five vacation rentals, one of which is eight bedrooms and nearly 5,000 square feet. In addition, she manages homes for clients of her own. She has become one of the most successful vacation rental owners that I know of because she knows what works for her. Her style is unique, and her guests know what to expect when they rent from her, regardless of the property size.

I have another client who buys vacation rentals strictly for investment. He has no plans to stay in the property and, in fact, cannot stay in it due to the IRS rules that come along with the pool of money he is using to invest. He is using a self-directed IRA to purchase his real estate investments, and the income grows tax-free or tax-deferred inside the fund. In this case, a custodian from the IRA company buys the property on his behalf. He is not able to stay at the property or do any personal work on the property; he must hire out all of the services required to operate the vacation rental, but the tax benefits for him are phenomenal. When we are searching for these homes, we are not looking so much for comfort or amenities but for a great entry price. Since he uses a management company and must pay them a fee, we make sure there is enough margin for profit. We are primarily looking for functional properties with a proven track record where comfort and upgrades can be added with income earned from the property.

The last example I like to use is a friend of mine from Arkansas. His name is Richard Carraway, and you'll get introduced to him in a later chapter. Richard is part country boy, part businessman and one-hundred-percent storybook. I could listen to this guy tell stories for hours, and believe me, he could keep you there. He and his wife, Jessica, are CPAs and operate a successful practice. They are also smart real estate investors. Their whole nightly rental business plan is built on what Richard calls "Wow Factor." If the property has Wow Factor and can, buy his calculations, be paid off in 5-7 years with the income earned, it's a go.

Maybe you are only looking at six-bedroom homes because that is the business plan that you've adopted, or perhaps you are getting your feet wet with a two-bedroom. The benefit you have, is that you are specific about what you want to buy and will be therefore focus on that sector of the market. This determination and focus will allow you to act quickly when the right one comes your way.

The people I've worked with who know exactly what they want before they buy are, by far, my most successful clients. They have strong criteria that they rarely waver on, and this is the first step to buying a successful vacation rental. Understanding how you are going to use the property, whether for personal use and management, strict investment or some combination in between, will give you a head start on the road to success because you'll know exactly what you need to buy.

Step #2 Look for an opportunity, not a deal

You should always be looking for a deal, but if this is all you are used to doing, you could miss out when you come strolling into the nightly rental world. You've heard the saying that there are three rules to real estate: location, location, location. In my experience, this is just not true. The rules should be: location, location, timing, because timing is everything. Think about it. If you closed on the best real estate deal in the best location in New Orleans on August 22, 2005, Hurricane Katrina would have come the next day and changed everything.

If you bought real estate almost anywhere in 2007, I bet you lost some equity. Timing is everything, and it can work in your favor, as well. I had a client buy a villa on a mediocre golf course that got bought out by some big money investors who landed an annual contract with the Senior PGA tournament. The month after we closed on them, the rest of the inventory in that neighborhood evaporated. Everybody wanted one. No one knew it was going to happen; it was luck, but it was good luck and was bought at the right time.

Here is another example: I recently completed a purchase for a client who was new to the world of vacation rentals. We had been working with him for a while, so he knew what he wanted. He was looking for a lakefront vacation rental. These are pretty rare in my neck of the woods. Even better, it was "turnkey," which means furnished down to the forks. It was ready to rent; just bring your toothbrush. The best property, by far, for a new vacation rental buyer is, without a doubt, a fully-furnished, fully-operational, established rental with bookings. This way you are able to bypass the set-up phase and can take advantage of the clientele and cash deposits that the previous owner has worked hard to develop. The opportunity to get started this way was huge. We found, for this investor, a vacation rental that was literally steps away from the lake. It was fully furnished and had over $13,000 of cash deposits that the seller was ready to let go, and, in addition to all of this, had a vacant lot right next door. The problem was, this buyer was looking for a deal and was used to being a stern negotiator in all of his business dealings. When he couldn't get the property for $30,000 below market value, he almost walked until we pointed out to him that the opportunity to own this property far outweighed the deal he wanted to get. The operating income on the property alone exceeded $50,000 per year, and he would be getting an extra lot that he could build on or use to add amenities. When he finally saw the opportunity, he completed the purchase and is now exceeding the income earned by the previous owner.

Another thing to be very cautious of when buying a vacation rental is a foreclosure or short sale. If the property is not even paying for itself and is causing a hardship for the existing owner, then why do you want it? If it is not renting, you want to know why, and you owe it to yourself to start asking some direct questions. Buying a vacation rental is not like buying any other piece of investment real estate. There are many more factors to pay attention to that will determine your success, and purchase price is only one of them. You are much better off finding a motivated seller than a distressed property because the transactions have shorter escrows (close faster) and there are no bank board members or bankrupt courts involved. These distressed properties can work and shouldn't be avoided, rather they should be approached with an additional layer of caution.

It is very important when buying a vacation rental to learn the real estate market where you will be making your purchase. Know what you are buying before you buy it. Do some market research ahead of time so you don't miss out on an opportunity when you see one. Many people wait until they come to town to start looking around, but with the technology tools available today, you can practically learn any market in your pajamas. Many agents provide the opportunity to search the MLS from their company websites or to save some listings in a personal listing cart. You can be notified of price drops on your favorite properties and begin to see how long properties stay on the market and at what price. Without this knowledge, you will never know what you are missing out on. This is the kind of smart tactic that will help build your confidence and allow you to act on an opportunity when it comes available.

Step #3 Decide the size of the money machine you want (and can afford)

The reason I compare a nightly rental to a money machine is to help you focus on what is most important about the purchase. This is more of a commercial purchase rather than a residential one, and, for that reason, you need to approach it with a business mind rather than a real estate mind. The commodity of your business is not the real estate; that is simply the location of the business. The commodity of your business is heads in beds, and that is really the name of the game. The more heads you have in beds, the more dollars you will have at the end of the year. So, as you begin to become an expert on the vacation rental business by following my plan in this book, you will start planning your purchase, your amenities, extras and comfort items, not on what you think people want, but on what will bring the most quality reviews to your home based on feedback and proven techniques. If you only focus on location, you are leaving many of your success factors unattended.

Here is a real-life illustration. I had a client who wanted a two-bedroom, two-bathroom lake view condo. It was a beautiful condo at a "deal" price of $175,000. He was going to put 25% down on the purchase ($43,750) and rent it out to make gobs of cash flow. He kept saying that surely everyone wants a beautiful lake view condo to stay in. He felt that he absolutely would be able to charge a premium price for the lake view. It's true, you can charge a premium for lake view, but there were two success factors he was not considering. First, he had not considered that the HOA dues were extremely high, and second, the property did not have nice beds or TVs in every room. Meanwhile, another client of mine across town was looking at a $65,000 golf condo and was ready to put down 25% ($16,250). It was the same square footage in a similar location but no view. What this seasoned vacation rental buyer knew was that comfortable beds and TVs in every room were highly-favored and marketable amenities. Not to mention, the lower purchase price allowed him to book the property at a lower per night rate.

Here is a comparison of two properties:

At the end of the year, the investor who bought the golf condo was able to book more nights because he paid attention to the success factors of the business: What am I offering? Does my

Lake View

Purchase Cost	$ 175,000.00
Loan amount	$ 140,000.00
Principal and Interest at 4%	$ 668.39
Ave Per night Rate	$ 130.00
Gross Income	$ 21,320.00
Annual debt service	$ 8,020.00
Taxes	$ 700.00
Insurance	$ 1,000.00
HOA dues	$ 3,000.00
Advertising	$ 1,500.00
Repairs	$ 500.00
Supplies	$ 500.00
Utilities	$ 3,000.00
Misc	$ 500.00
Net operating Income (cash flow before tax)	$ 2,600.00
Cash invested	$ 34,000.00
*Cash on Cash return	7.6%

* Example only - not a guarantee of a return

property have the things that guests are looking for in this market? What are some of my common expenses, because no matter how many nights I book, these expenses will cut into my bottom line. The most important question you can ask yourself with regard to home amenities is, "How much more per night can I earn by having this amenity?" If it does not make your money machine pump out more money, it may not be worth the added purchase price.

Small Golf Condo

Purchase Cost:	$ 85,000.00
Loan amount:	$ 68,000.00
Principal and Interest at 4%	$ 325.00
Ave Per night Rate:	$ 120.00
Gross Income:	$ 19,680.00
Annual debt service:	$ 3,896.00
Taxes:	$ 600.00
Insurance:	$ 1,000.00
HOA dues:	$ 3,000.00
Advertising:	$ 1,500.00
Repairs:	$ 500.00
Supplies:	$ 500.00
Utilities:	$ 3,000.00
Misc:	$ 500.00
Net operating Income (cash flow before tax)	$ 5,184.00
Cash invested:	$ 17,000.00
*Cash on Cash return	30%

* Example only - not a guarantee of a return

As an investor in the nightly rental real estate business, you should stop thinking about how many properties you own and start thinking about the number of bedrooms you own. The client who was interested in the lake view condo was dead set on lake view. We showed him how, with only two bedrooms, his earnings potential was limited. However, since he had the funds for the lake view price range, we showed him scenarios for a purchase of a three-bedroom. He could earn an extra $8,000 - $14,000 per year renting it out. That third bedroom was a huge asset, way more of an asset than the lake view. Not only could he charge a bit more per night, but another family could come in and split the nightly rent three ways instead of two. This would make the property appealing if the economy shifted. It is more economical for the family and more income for the owner. Some people just want a lake view, and that is ok because they are clear on what they want, but if rate of return is first on your priority list, this is a strategy you should consider.

In a condo, you can see how the fixed expenses, like advertising and HOA dues, do not change that much, but the extra bedroom adds powerful income potential.

As much time as you spend looking for the property, you need to carefully analyze the amount of income you can earn on the number of bedrooms versus your expenses and compare all of this to the amount of cash you invest. The most important number when buying a vacation rental is not the purchase price, it is your rate of return. Rate of return is everything. It is the one statistic that can determine the

2 BR CONDO

Purchase Cost:	$ 65,000.00
Loan amount:	$ 52,000.00
Principal and Interest at 4%	$ 248.26
Ave Per night Rate:	$ 99.00
Gross Income:	$ 16,236.00
Annual debt service:	$ 2,979.00
Taxes:	$ 600.00
Insurance:	$ 1,000.00
HOA dues:	$ 3,000.00
Advertising:	$ 1,500.00
Repairs:	$ 500.00
Supplies:	$ 500.00
Utilities:	$ 3,000.00
Misc:	$ 500.00
Net operating income (cash flow before tax)	$ 2,657.00
Cash invested:	$ 13,000.00
*Cash on Cash return	20%

* Example only - not a guarantee of a return

health (or potential health) of your investment. Don't
ask: what property do I want to buy, instead ask: is a two-bedroom business model or a six-bedroom business model right for my financial situation and investment goals? Here is a formula to help you determine your rate of return:

3 BR CONDO	
Purchase Cost	$ 90,000.00
Loan amount	$ 72,000.00
Principal and Interest at 4%	$ 343.74
Ave Per night Rate	$ 130.00
Gross Income	$ 21,320.00
Annual debt service	$ 4,124.88
Taxes	$ 700.00
Insurance	$ 1,100.00
HOA dues	$ 3,000.00
Advertising	$ 1,500.00
Repairs	$ 500.00
Supplies	$ 500.00
Utilities	$ 3,000.00
Misc	$ 500.00
Net operating Income (cash flow before tax)	$ 6,395.12
Cash invested	$ 18,000.00
*Cash on Cash return	35%

* Example only - not a guarantee of a return

GROSS OPERATING INCOME (GOI) - EXPENSES = NET OPERATING INCOME (NOI)

NOI - DEBT SERVICE = CASH FLOW

There are other factors you can add to help you achieve a true rate of return, such as principle reduction, tax savings and depreciation to help you get a true picture. Do not ever add appreciation to the property to your rate of return; this is speculation, not investing. Speculation is when you buy something and hope it goes up in value. Investing is making money the day you buy it. If the property appreciates, consider it a bonus. Do not ever buy a property in the hopes that it will appreciate; your money machine should be able to spit money out on its own today without the hope of any future conditions. If it does not, it is not a good money machine.

With this strategy, you can compare real estate to other types of investing. Now that you are asking yourself, "How much principle do I want to invest and what is my rate of return?" you go into the purchase as a true business person. You can now compare a real estate return to a stock market or bond return. If you can earn a better rate of return in a vacation rental than you can in your BRIC EFT, by all means, consider it. With this type of investment, you can go on vacation, use your investment, treat your family. Kids grow up fast and make kids of their own. Make memories with your investment money. You can't have much fun with your quarterly earnings statement from your 401K. Who on earth can sit in a room with their family and their 401K statement and have a good time?

Step #4 Do some private detective work

Now that you've decided how you want to use the property, and you have studied the real estate market and understand what your investment goals are, it's time to grab some coffee and sit down at your computer. Put on your super sleuth hat, and follow these instructions.

Find out how many "peak season" nights are in your market. Peak season can be considered any night that falls in the high-traffic times of the tourist season where you are buying. You can also count any holiday nights as peak season. Add these up, and if you can get somewhere between ninety and one hundred nights, then you are on the right track. You must rely on your peak season nights to help pay the expenses of your property. It's the off peak times where you make your profit. You will also want to discover if there are any "dark" nights, also known as the off season. These are nights where tourist traffic has all together stopped, and you need to know how many off season nights there are so you can accurately estimate your rate of return.

Next, you absolutely must spend some time browsing some vacation rental owner websites to discover what properties rent for. Get a good picture of what you can

BAD Example	GOOD Example	
100 Nights	90 Nights - PEAK	60 Nights - OFF PEAK
(based on what you think it will rent for)	(Based on 100 in your market)	(Based on data from owner's call)
$300 per night	$300 per night	$225 per night
(based on an average)	(based on an average)	(based on an average)
$30,000	$40,500	
(gross operating income for your calculations)	(gross operating income for your calculations)	

charge per season and compare the nights in each season with the rental rate. Keep separate totals so you can get a more accurate estimate.

Not everyone does this next step, but we always encourage it. Pick up the phone and call someone else who owns in the area that you are buying. Find out if they are happy. Are they doing well? Are the amenities in good shape? Call the homeowners association. Is the HOA strong or defunct? Is it a good community of owners?

How are nightly rentals viewed in the community? Are they welcomed, tolerated, or is there a lawsuit pending to get rid of them altogether? These are things you need to know before you buy, and you cannot always rely on a real estate agent to know these things. It is your job to do your own due diligence, and it is an agent's job to help you. If you do this step, be sure you call more than one person, if possible, so you don't call the one disgruntled guy in the community and miss out on a great opportunity. It happens. In my experience, the owners are more than happy to have a conversation with you.

Finally, you should call the county planning and zoning department to make sure nightly rentals are permitted and, if so, what the approval or transfer process is. This is an important step that, if overlooked, could have devastating consequences.

Step #5 Write an offer

There are two questions you should ask yourself before you write an offer on real estate: what is my exit strategy and am I going to regret making the payment each month? First, if you know your exit strategy, it will help guide you as you make decisions on the purchase. Why pay the interest rate on a thirty-year fixed loan if you are going to sell in five years? You might be better off paying a lower interest rate and get a seven-year ARM (Adjustable Rate Mortgage). If you are going to hold the property for a number of years, then you will want to buy more durable furniture. If all else fails, you will want to know if you can at least get out of the property what you put into it. Second, if you don't think you are going to enjoy making the payment, meaning if you are not going to use and enjoy the property yourself or you don't think you will be proud or successful with your investment, then don't buy it. Some initial anxiety is normal, but if you are waking up sweating, you may want to check in with your thought process. The answer to these questions will help you determine if you are ready to make an offer.

Your prior research and some good comparable sales from a real estate agent will be able to help you determine an offer price, earnest money and a closing date. Be sure, of course, to protect your earnest money. Give yourself adequate time to perform all necessary inspections and an appraisal. Here are some important categories to consider when you are writing an offer on a vacation rental.

INVENTORY LIST

Don't be vague. Ambiguity is the enemy to a real estate contract. When you are buying a fully-furnished vacation rental, be sure to list every item of furniture and personal property that will convey with the purchase. I also like to take pictures and make them part of the inventory addendum. This way, no one can swap out a TV or refrigerator. I've seen it happen. Or a seller will say that they were planning on keeping all of the décor. Is décor furniture? What about lamps? Are lamps furniture or décor? The point is, if you list the lamp and go so far to take a picture of it, your contract will be stronger because it is very specific. Furthermore, before writing the inventory list you should ask the seller if they have any personal property or special furniture or décor items that are personal to them that they do not want to sell with the property. This way you can have a conversation about it first, address it and there will be fewer surprises later.

ADDENDUM FOR TRANSFER OF BOOKINGS

If you don't address this up front, you do not know the true value of the property. If the property comes with $20,000 worth of booking deposits, it is arguably worth more than an identical property without them. The real estate has a value, and the booking deposits have a value; make sure you consider both before making an offer, and make sure you ask for the bookings when you do. When you are ready to write an offer, ask the seller for an itemized list of bookings with a breakdown in the following categories: name of party, total rent, rent collected to date, rent outstanding, taxes collected, and cleaning fees collected. This way you know exactly what you are getting, and if the seller wants to keep a booking fee or a percentage of the rent as a term of the sale, then you can be sure to only apply that percentage to the rent and not the tax or cleaning fee.

You will also want to spell out who will manage the existing bookings. Will you manage them or will the seller manage them? If the seller manages them, you might check with your insurance company see if you need to make them an additional insured party on your policy while they are managing the bookings. If you manage them, then you want to get the complete contact information of each renter so you can reach out to them individually to let them know that you are the new property manager, and should they have any questions they can contact you. This addendum should also spell out that the current rental agreements, terms and cancellation policies have already been set and that whoever manages the bookings under the new ownership will honor these rental contracts to the letter.

TRANSFER OF TRADEMARKS OR NICKNAMES

If you are buying an established vacation rental, then be sure that you transfer any registered trademarks. If the trademarks or nicknames are unregistered, then at the very least, you will want some written permission from the seller to be able to use these as long as you own the property. You will need to be able to convey ownership of these trademarks or nicknames to anyone you sell the property to. While you are on this step, be sure to ask if there are any websites that can be conveyed to you or contact lists of past customers. These are not that commonly transferred, but it is worth asking. If the seller has the property in an LLC, you can, in some cases, transfer the LLC and all the applicable assets.

INSPECTIONS

Here are some common inspections you may want to consider:

Home Inspection – This is commonly a visual inspection of the structure, electrical, plumbing and mechanical systems. This person may recommend further inspections by a specialist if necessary.

Septic/Wastewater – This is a visual inspection of the septic system and lateral lines. More invasive inspections can be performed at your request.

Well Inspections – This involves a chemical test of the water to make sure it is safe for drinking. It is usually tested for nitrates and coliform bacteria.

Radon – This is a test for a naturally occurring, radioactive, colorless, odorless gas.

Title work – This should reveal if the property is transferrable or has any liens or back taxes due.

Appraisal – This is an opinion of value of your home from a certified appraiser.

Condo Resale Certificate (if applicable) – This will show pending assessments and overall solvency of the HOA.

Sex Offender Registration – This is a list of residences of known sex offenders.

Termite Inspection – This is a visual inspection for active or past termite activity in a home.

Bed Bug Inspection - This is not a huge concern, but it is definitely a step you do not want to miss when buying a nightly rental. Bed Bugs are not easy to get rid of. They are a costly beast to irradiate, and this is not a burden you want to take on as a new owner. In addition to the cost of treatment, it could result in lost bookings or revenue while the property is closed. Once you own a property, be sure to add this to your checklist. Set up a plan with a pest control company to have your home regularly checked and treated; prevention is worth everything in this case.

So, there you have it. There might be more to do than you originally thought. I don't want you to feel overwhelmed; I want you to feel smart and confident because if you have done these things then you are light years ahead of the learning curve. These tips and tactics have come out of real-life transactions that I've been a part of, and I'd like for you to have the benefit of my mistakes. It will be fun and very exciting to find your next vacation rental purchase. I hope having done these extras will help you go into the transaction with more confidence.

Chapter Four

Six Simple Secrets to Setting up Your Vacation Rental

Setting up your vacation rental is a bit like deciding to sail around the world. The adventure is full of excitement and energy, there are many possibilities and who knows who you'll meet along the way. But, locked inside the lower deck of your dreamy fun ship is a treasure map that, if you ignore, it will find you castaway, cross eyed and babbling to a volleyball named Wilson. It will seem like a daunting task, especially if you are starting from scratch. This chapter is built by those who have sailed around the world many times. It comes with good advice and checklists so you know what to bring with you on your journey. We will help you plot a clear course, navigate the danger zones and get you sailing.

Budget enough time to set up your rental

Time is an important factor in setting up your vacation rental. Every day that you spend setting it up is a day that you could have rented the property. Setting up is lost revenue, but it is an important part of the business that should be given a dedicated block of time. I've seen people fail miserably at both ends of this spectrum. One ambitious couple bought a completely empty, brand new home to use as a rental and only budgeted one weekend to get the property set up. The busy weekend included picking out furniture with rush delivery. They worked eighteen hours a day, shopping, setting up services, moving furniture and in the end they didn't finish and had wait over a month before they could come back down to complete the setup on another weekend they were off work. That was an entire month of lost revenue.

Another couple I worked with were tax professionals and were very busy at the start of the year. They closed on the property early in the year because it was a good deal, and they didn't want to pass it up. Because it was full-on tax season, they were covered up. They made a few attempts to get away and set up, but in the end it was May before they could really sink their teeth into it. Not because they were lazy, but because business came first. In the end, it was the middle of July before they began advertising, and by that time they had missed over a month-and-a-half of peak season nights. They did, however, get it done, and they reaped the benefit of the end of peak season and were ready to capture all of the fall and Christmas season. However, it was a long, drawn-out process that was on their minds longer than it needed to be. The takeaway here is: buy the home with your setup plan already in place. Gather the help you are going to need, and don't feel bad about bribing babysitters and friends to help you move furniture and make beds. These gracious souls work for pizza and a chance to stay at the home rent-free for a weekend.

This is not a task you should take lightly. If you do, it will create stress, anxiety and more work. If you treat this like a business, make a plan and set aside a block of time, it will go smooth, and you will enjoy it. So how much time do you need? The bigger the property, the more time you will need, of course, but in our experience you should be able get it all done in one week as long as no repairs or painting are needed. If you are looking at a two or three-bedroom, you can get away with about five days, but for a six or seven-bedroom, I'd budget ten days.

 TIP: Spend wisely on furniture. Find good, clean deals. Everything doesn't need to be new; however, beds should be, if possible.

When you block your time, if possible, try not to be in the middle of another project or life event. My wife, Kelly, and I always pick the worst times to set up a rental. I suppose we love adventure. We found a builder closeout on a five-bedroom that was too good to pass on. It came with some furniture, but not much. It was January, so it was our off season, but as we will learn later in the book, January is when many people start booking larger properties (five or more bedrooms) for the summer, so we had a sense of urgency to set it up, take pictures and begin marketing it. This major setup and purchase happened just after we had our third baby. Kelly was in the hospital spending time with our baby son, and we were accommodating family and guests. Anyone who's had children knows that when Momma is recovering in the hospital with a new baby, Daddy begins to realize how little he actually did for the other kids and finally understands the power and depths of a mother's job. Between feeding and entertaining everyone, coordinating the setup, with daddy daycare in full force, I found myself at midnight cussing at a put-together-yourself TV stand with two hungry kids still awake. In a daze of parts A, B, C and tiny pictures of screws, I looked up and saw my two-year-old son, wild eyed, ramming a steak knife in to the carpet. It was at that moment when I realized we'd taken on a bit too much. We got through it. Six days later, Kelly and I were shopping for kitchen wares with two kids in tow and a baby in a sling. I do understand that if we all waited for life events to stop before we set out to conquer the world, none of us would ever accomplish anything; life just keeps coming at you. Give yourself a reason to go for it instead of an excuse not to, and put some careful thought into your timing. This way you will control your action plan rather than letting the setup control you.

At this point in the game, it is a good idea to plan for a year of operation. Decide how long setup will take you so you can go ahead and advertise your first day of availability. While you are doing your setup, schedule some time to interview a few cleaning and handyman companies at the property. Schedule your TV subscription and internet, and make sure it all works before your first guests arrive. Take this time to schedule your off season deep cleans, touch ups and property upgrades to make sure you are not taking peak season time to do things that can wait until the off season.

 TIP: When you paint the Interior of a vacation home, be sure to use a satin paint instead of flat. It is much easier to touch up and keep clean.

Resist the urge to innovate

I'm a huge fan of the entrepreneurial spirit and good old-fashioned Yankee ingenuity, but for heaven's sakes don't do it, at least not until you are an experienced vacation rental owner. The words to live by at this stage of the game are to follow the model of properties that work, then add your signature. Your signature is the theme you choose to decorate the home with, the quality and luxury level of beds and linens, the bear statue in the front yard, the quote you decide to stencil on the wall, the extras you will provide that no one else does. This is staying in the model and adding your signature. Your signature also includes any ideas you have about deals you want to make with local restaurants or attractions to cross-promote. Heads in beds is what drives your economic engine, and this should be the focus of your business model. You should specialize in getting heads in beds and getting them to return to your property. Hot tubs and pool tables are good examples of amenities that can add great value to your property. They fit into the business model and can be used to your unique advantage.

So what is an example of too much innovation? Offering horses, boats and jet skis as a part of your rental package is an example of taking on too much, especially if you are new at this. Why not let a horse rancher be an expert at running the ranch or a marina be an expert at renting motor boats? I love watching business people explore new possibilities, and I believe a vacation rental dedicated to people who love horses, who can bring them and care for them and enjoy time with their animals is an amazing idea. Equestrian rentals work and could be lucrative in your area. If you are convicted to do this, then you should. However, if you just love horses, why not try first setting up one of your bedrooms with horse décor; let that be your signature and see if that does not satisfy you first.

Don't buy everything you love

When you shop for your furniture and inventory, remember that there will be other people in your home, and most of the time they will be very respectful, but sometimes people forget to put the strap on the Wii remote. We learned this the hard way. Grandpa had just bought his favorite TV, a 46-inch Flat Screen Sony HD TV with 1080p, and within thirty days, it was shattered. It is extremely rare for things like this to happen, but if you are in the business long enough, it will. It is important to view the items in this home not as your personal property, but as pieces of wood and cloth, tools and devices to help you get more nights booked. If you want an amazing TV, go buy one for yourself and put your old one in your vacation rental. It is ok love the amazing lamps you found, or the headboard or quilt. I'm just saying, don't get attached to it because if you do, when it is your turn to say in your home, you may be disappointed. You will be offended that people don't take care of your stuff as good as you do, but isn't that something you already know? You could increase your happiness by setting up your home, with stylish and durable furniture and décor and nice TVs.

If you want your personal items in your home, then set up an owner's closet. Take one of the closets of the home, put a lock on it and make it yours. Go so far as to put a sign on it that says "Owner's Closet" if for no other reason than to inspire curiosity as to what's behind that door. Everything that you love, use and enjoy when you are on vacation can be brought out of your owner's closet and carefully locked up when you are away.

When you are shopping for furniture, it is easier

to buy everything from a large retailer who can sell you everything at once. If you are a price shopper, you may not want to do it this way, but if time is important to you, then try to go to one place where you can buy all of your furniture, appliances, electronics and some décor. The benefit here is that the retailer will show up with all of your stuff, move it in for you, set up the furniture and take the boxes and packaging with them when they go. Don't skimp on comfortable mattresses. If you have a fold-out couch, put a memory foam topper on the top of the mattress. Those mattresses can get pretty thin, and the memory foam is a nice touch. You may want to protect those nice mattresses with a waterproof cover and/or a cover that fully encloses the mattress to prevent pests. I've also found it very easy to order blinds for a new home by using the window treatment department of a big chain hardware store. You can contact the store near your rental and have someone come out and measure all of the windows, then you can go to your local store in your hometown to make selections. Once you know the item numbers you want, you can call the store near your rental and order what you want by the color and model so there is no confusion. If you can avoid putting up blinds yourself, you can save almost an entire day of setup time.

 TIP: If possible, have an electric outlet in your owner's closet. Many people keep a small fridge with condiments so you don't have to re-purchase this every time. It is not recommended to keep open containers in your vacation rental.

Find a good cleaning company

This is the most important part of your team. Your cleaning company or cleaning person should be experienced, reliable and friendly. The quality and feedback you will receive from your guests will be a direct result of the quality of your cleaning company and the strength of your partnership with them.

The best case scenario, whether you hire a company or an individual, is to have the same person clean your home each time. This way the person finds a groove and routine that will help them clean the home faster. This is important when doing quick changes. Quick changes are when one guest leaves and the other arrives on the same day. You will set the check-in times and the check-out times, and it will be up to you to enforce those times. If you do not enforce those times and people leave late, or if you allow people to check-in early from time to time, you are making your job as a property manager significantly harder. You now have to remember which guest you've allowed to do what and now have to adjust your cleaning team to every whim of each unique guest. Please listen to this advice: create a firm policy on check-in and check-out because it will save your bacon.

If you are using the same person to clean your home, not only will this person become efficient at the job, but they will learn to easily recognize things that are out of place or missing. When you get the call from your cleaning team and have an issue to resolve, because you have strict check in and check out times with plenty of margin, you now know exactly how much time you have to have to resolve the issue. Many new owners want loose check-in and check-out times because they want to make the guest comfortable, and this is important for sure. Other owners want to offer more competitive check-in and check-out times because they believe it will help get bookings. Eventually, though, a day will come along when you wish you had more time. Talk to your cleaner, find out how much time they need and work with them to find a balance that works for both of you. A typical check-in is after 4 p.m., and a typical check-out is before 10 a.m.

Cleaning a nightly rental has the potential to be a negative job because there will always be dirt. No matter how many times you clean a place, someone will always be able to find more dirt that you missed. Kelly ran a cleaning company for many years; she started this business during the 2008 recession because there is always dirt, and there are always people who do not want to clean it. It is a recession-proof business. My advice here is that when you have a guest complaint or notice something that is not done to your satisfaction, when you talk to your cleaner, be honest but be nice. Remember, your cleaner is your valued partner, and you don't want one guest to mess that up for you. There will be many times when your cleaner will do odd jobs or get you out of a jam, so be sure to appreciate them during those times. I recommend paying your cleaning person well; when you find a good cleaner, he or she will be worth every penny. One way to help resolve many cleaning issues is to create a cleaning checklist that is specific to your property. This way you can be clear in your expectations of a cleaner, and you both sign off on it.

A good scenario with a cleaning company with employees is for them to carry Worker's Compensation and general liability insurance and have them be bonded.

This is not always economical for a cleaning person who cleans only a few properties. If nothing else, it is best if this person can have a general liability policy for accidents. We've prepared some questions here to help you select a cleaning company that is best for you:

1. Are you flexible to do last-minute cleanings for last-minute bookings?
2. Do you have insurance?
3. Do you do extras such as clean the grill?
4. Can you clean ceiling fans, vents, and air filters once a month?
5. If you have an employee clean for you, can someone do a "double check" of the property to make sure all the i's are dotted and the t's are crossed?
6. Can you have the same person clean every time?
7. Are you comfortable with feedback so that we can have open and respectful communication about things I may notice?
8. Can you invoice me once a month for cleanings?
9. Can you text me after cleanings are done and let me know if there are any problems immediately?
10. Can you let me know when supplies are running low?
11. Do you clean or spot clean windows?

 TIP: Remember your check-in and check-out times are not just for the cleaning company; this time is needed to manage any issues that come up during a quick change.

Keep things separate and organized

You want to have one property manager and only one. During a time of transition, Kelly and I were both attempting to tackle the management of a property. She and I were running in opposite directions, and we double booked the property. This was kind of a worst-case scenario for us because, at the time, we only had one property. We ended up finding an open property for this group, made sure it was nicer than ours, and we paid the difference. It was the least we could do, and it was how we would have wanted to have been treated. The point here is that multiple managers can do more harm than good.

It is also a good idea, during the setup phase, to create a unique email for your property or business. If you think you may someday have multiple properties, then plan ahead and think of a creative name for yourself or business. If you create a separate email account for each individual property, you may be able to add future value to the sale of your property by transferring that email account and list of past clients to the new owner.

It's also a good idea to set up a unique bank account for the property. This way you can track your cash flow in real time. Then, if you pass off the management of the property to someone else, they only have access to the funds in the operating account of that one property. Furthermore, if you choose to contract a merchant services or credit card company, you can have those funds directly deposited into this account, and it just makes things easier to manage. If you are co-mingling the funds from different properties, it may be hard to determine which properties are paying for themselves. The goal is to get the property to pay for its own bills and to cut you a dividend check at the regular interval you decide. Some people decide to have all of the assets of the property, as well as the property itself, placed into an LLC. This can offer you some good protection if it is done correctly, but you'll also have to change a few things about the way you operate your business to make sure you can take advantage of the LLC protection. The best thing to do here is to consult with an attorney who knows LLC law in your state and get advice on the finer points of this. I'll go a bit more into entity selection in a later chapter.

 TIP: Check with your cable provider before buying TVs. There is no point in paying the money for 1080p TVs if the cable comes through in 720p.

Setting up your utilities and services

The question I get asked most often here is: should I go with ultra-premium or basic services? The rule of thumb is to do at least everything that a hotel does, and then a bit more. Definitely provide a land phone line, towels, extra blankets, and a TV service with a few channels for kids. It is also a good idea to provide coffee, a hair dryer, an ironing board, soaps/shampoos, laundry detergent, and Wi-Fi. If you have all of this, you will get more bookings and some good reviews. Then you can amp it up a bit more and provide a pack-n-play, high chair, terrycloth robes, a desk and printer, a DVD or Blu-ray Player, a movie library with kid movies and a video game system. If you have these premium items, your reviews and overall guest satisfaction will increase dramatically.

TIP: Strongly consider adding a landline. You will be surprised how many people use it. It is a good safety feature to have.

You really don't need a fancy lock. A good $20 coded Master Lock will work, but you will want to be sure to get down there and change that code from time to time for safety reasons. Plus, you rely on your guest not losing the key. The best scenario is a simple key code lock so you don't have to worry about keys. These locks can have multiple codes and can be changed easily. The best thing you can do is get a premium lock that connects to your Wi-Fi. In this case, you will be notified when guests arrive or if the door has been left ajar. You can give unique codes to your cleaning company or to a handy man so you know who has been in and out of your property. There is some peace of mind that comes with seeing your cleaner's code come through at 10:15 when you know the guests have just left at 10:00, and you have new guests arriving at 4:00. You can even get the whole home system now that allows you to control the lights and thermostat if you want. This can help you cut your utility bill by making sure the thermostat and lights are adjusted when guests leave. It can also help you adjust the temperature and turn a light on before guests arrive. These systems are great for home security in areas with an off season to help it appear as if someone is home. You have many fun choices, and you'll discover what is right for you. Be sure to set up these new services during the week you are there so you can test them and make sure they work before your first guests arrive.

Chapter Five

Marketing, Promotions & You

Before you start operating your vacation rental, you have to get heads in beds. This is the most important chapter in the book because heads in beds is the name of the game. Without this, you have no business; you just have a very expensive second home. The first thing you should do is select a name for your home. Don't skip this step; it is not silly. It gives your home an identity and will help guests instantly recognize what you are offering and help them find you again in the future. People want to stay at The Lucky Day Lodge; they don't want to stay at a four-bedroom cabin in the woods. A four-bedroom cabin in the woods is the setting for most teenage horror flicks, but The Lucky Day Lodge, now that would be a fun family getaway. Plus, it's easy to remember! We've always had a lot of fun voting on the best name. It's a lot like naming your children. Everyone has an opinion. You get tons of horrible suggestions, but it's much less stressful because it won't grow up to become Senator Obi Wan.

There are so many different avenues you can take when marketing your home: Facebook, Twitter, Instagram, YouTube, Google +, blogging and general SEO are all great tools to use, but these should not be your main focus at first. All of these sites should get some of your time, but they should point all traffic to your main website. Your main website is where you will conduct most of your business, manage your calendar and capture your leads. If you only focus the three things I'm about to tell you and never spend a minute on Facebook, you will still succeed. What I'm trying to say is: don't get distracted by Facebook and all those sites that can be daunting to master. This is encouraging because you do not have to master social media to master nightly rentals. Stay focused on building a presence in a place where people are already shopping for a place to stay. For all of the resources and marketing tools available, you should concentrate on three main things: site management, inquiries and reviews.

Web Management

Web management refers to the main website you will use to book your property. There are many international and regional travel sites available to the vacation rental owner. You could even build your own personal website, but then you will be responsible for driving traffic to your site. This is not impossible, but it takes time and dollars. You are better off starting with a listing on one of these international sites where many of the vacation travelers are already looking. Many of these sites charge a percentage to book your home and do not charge an initial listing fee. I recommend that you look for a website with high vacation traffic and a reasonable listing fee. A listing fee is something you can budget for; it is a fixed expense on your business plan. A percentage is more like a tax that never goes away. You will end up paying more if you pay a percentage on your main website. Whatever you decide to use, make sure it is easy to interact with and that there is tech support available if you have questions. If you use the HomeAway family of sites, including HomeAway.com, VRBO.com and VacationRentals.com, you will get the opportunity to use one calendar and a pretty handy back-end management system. The HomeAway people know what they are doing and are primarily responsible for the break-out of this industry. Their tech tools and websites are geared to make it easier for the owner and the renter. Also, look into sites like Airbnb and FlipKey to help round out your arsenal.

Pictures are everything

When you are listing your vacation rental on various websites, the one thing that you can do that will have the most positive impact is to take amazing pictures and put as many as you can in the listing. Pictures are the first impression a guest has of your property, and if you can't even take a good main image, guests will wonder what else are you slacking on. Pictures are the tires on car, the shoes on the business woman, the gel in a guy's hair. You may not think they are important, but everyone else does. Enhance them, crop them, but don't Photoshop the beach in the background. Be sure you are offering a true picture of your home. If you get the opportunity to get a listing and it is priced by the number of pictures you can add, then I always recommend to add the maximum number of pictures. Your advertising budget will be relatively low in this business compared to other industries, so max it out, and make your listings stand out with classy pictures. Don't just think about lighting and positioning of that empty bath tub. Go to some effort to fill it up with bubbles and light a candle next to it. You don't want to wait for the perfect sunset on the lake to put up your main image, but the day you see it, take that perfect picture and replace your existing image.

What I am stressing here is: don't just take pictures; put some thought into it and take *amazing* pictures. Your investment in this will pay dividends.

If you are a horrible photographer, use your resourcefulness to take on the challenge. Contact a professional photographer and offer a trade. Let their family stay in your home or offer to promote your photographer in your rental agreements or in your home. Many families love to get a professional family photo while they are on vacation.

 TIP: DO NOT PUT YOURSELF IN YOUR PICTURES. THE GOAL IS TO SHOW OFF YOUR PROPERTY, NOT YOUR LONG, FLOWING, BEAUTIFUL HAIR. OTHER PEOPLE IN YOUR PICTURES ARE LIKE A DIRTY FORK AT A RESTAURANT; IT REMINDS EVERYONE THAT SOMEONE ELSE'S LIPS HAVE TOUCHED IT.

Text and Headings

Your heading on your website is a powerful tool. It is the first text that most people will see, and it is your banner to get everyone's attention. We've always had a great deal of luck by keeping our nickname in our banner. As I mentioned before, this helps to brand your home and set it apart each time someone searches for your home. A home with a name, seems more like a business and seems to be more professionally run. Remember, it may not be just one family booking your home; often it is many families planning a vacation, and anything you can do to help other people identify your home is a good practice. Keeping your nickname in your banner does make it harder to say anything else because of the limited number of characters, so you will want to put one other selling point in there.

LUCKY DAY LODGE – NEW TVS IN EVERY ROOM, NEW BEDS!

LUCKY DAY LODGE – DEAL $$ - FOR REMAINING SEPT DAYS!

Keep it simple and to the point. What is the one thing your property has that sets it apart? Don't try to say it all in your heading because it can actually work against you. Here are two examples of people trying to give you too much information in too little space:

BECHFRNT 4 BED BEAUTY, WITH GMEROOM, SAUNA, NEW GRILL CLOSE TO THEMEPARK, EXTRA PARKING, WLK 2 POOL, CLNROOM

You still have the main body of your text to say everything you want to about your home. Be sure to do most of your selling in the first two sentences or at least in the first paragraph. Most people will not read the entire description, so keep the best parts of your home closer to the front of your listing text. Remember, this is an opportunity to see your home, not the city your home is in. It is not your job to sell your town; leave that to the Chamber of Commerce. If they are on your listing, they have already decided to come to the area. Use this precious "real estate" to talk about what your property has that no other property has. What extras do you offer? What deals are your offering? This is also your opportunity to stand out as an expert in your area. Talk about how close in proximity your home is from a grocery store, retail shopping, shows, the beach, hiking trails, marinas, theme parks or any other relevant attractions. If vacation-goers know you are an expert in this, they may lean toward you for some vacation advice.

Now you've added more value to their vacation than just being a place to stay; you are a trusted advisor. In each of the categories in this chapter, you will see just how important you are. You are almost as important as your property because there are hundreds of places to stay in any town, but if you make a friend or build trust, you will get that booking.

I would like to make one more important point about your text. Don't market what you can't control. Certainly you want to talk about any community pools, playgrounds or game rooms that may be available to your guests. However, if there is a community amenity that is available such as a clubhouse that is locked at random times or the workout equipment is broken all of the time, I'd remove those items from your listing text because it will only result in complaints and poor reviews. If you list it in your description of the property and it is unavailable or broken, it will reflect negatively on you and your per-night rental rate because you advertised it. Yet, if your focus is on primarily marketing your home and your guest finds some community amenities available to them, they will feel like it is above and beyond what they've paid for. Then, if someone wrecks a treadmill, you hopefully won't get any calls about it.

TIP: GET SOME BUSINESS CARDS PRINTED THAT INCLUDE YOUR PROPERTY NICKNAME, CONTACT INFO, PICTURE & WEBSITE. PUT A STACK IN THE HOME. YOUR GUESTS WILL TAKE ONE TO REMEMBER WHERE THEY STAYED, AND THEY WILL GIVE SOME OUT TO FRIENDS.

Pricing

Pricing is a careful balance. When in Rome, you should do as the Romans do. You'll have already done your research on the rate, so try to stay as comparable to other similar properties as you can. If you are in a community, you don't want to aggravate everyone else by undercutting them constantly. This usually ends in some else undercutting you, and eventually it drives the rates down for the entire community. Have some courage when pricing your home. Know your property's value, and let those undercutters book up first at those super low rates. Once they are all booked up, you will be able to book yours at your rate and come out ahead at the end of the year. Stay in the market, and be confident. If you do offer a deal, be sure to put a time limit on your deal price like this:

$25 OFF PER NIGHT FOR REMAINING OCT NIGHTS! MUST BOOK BY SEPT 30!

You can make pricing as complex or as simple as you want. You can offer a weekly and a nightly rate; you can offer weekday and weekend rates, and if you can learn how to adjust these seasonally, you can help your property earn a bit more. I have had the most success by offering one nightly rate, and it changes per season to one different nightly rate. We also raise the rates slightly for Holidays. Having one rate per season is beneficial because the less confusing it is for the guest and for you, the better your experience will be with the inquiry. Many inquires come in the evening, and you'll be responding to the inquiry from your smartphone, so be sure you can do the quick math. You take your one rate, add the tax and cleaning fee and any holiday or pet premiums and you have your calculation. VRBO and HomeAway offer the ability to respond to the e-mail inquiry on your dashboard which will automatically attach the quote for you. I recommend that if you do this, customize the template that you are sending to your potential renter. Remember, they are getting the exact same response from everyone else on that website, so personalize it! It will make the difference if they are deciding between your property and another one. If you are just starting out, keep the rates simple.

How much negotiation should you do on your rates? First, never negotiate your rate for Thanksgiving. In our experience, it has always booked very early. Even then, we still get calls begging for rumors of cancellations. Second, your peak season rates should not be negotiated until about thirty days before the start of the season. This is true, especially if you have a four-or-more-bedroom property. These properties book farther out, and the benefit of a guest booking early is that they can choose their vacation time. The value for them is to have the ability to choose the days they want. If you negotiate with them, you are leaving money on the table. The last-minute folks that wait 30 days or less to book their large family vacation are at your mercy, but your calendar may not fit theirs. If you slash your rates at this time, you now make your property incredibly valuable. What you find here, is that guests will actually adjust their family vacation to coincide with your available dates because your rates are better and because they waited too long.

You may get a lower rate per night, but you can ensure that you will have very few vacant peak season nights. By now, you know what the name of the game is.

Be careful of extremely high rates and extremely low rates. I don't judge people; I leave that to the Good Lord. Remember, this is your vacation home, and you do not have to rent to everyone. In moments of fear and anxiety, Kelly and I have offered ultra-low rates, and what we've found is that we get an ultra-low quality guest. I don't know what it is about the psychology of this, but many of the guests taking advantage of the ultra-low rate have taken advantage of us. Ultimately, the cost of operating and wear and tear of a property at a super low rate is infinitely higher. The same is true for super-high rates. There is another psychology lesson here I'm sure, but I'll speak from experience, not science. The absolute worst experiences we've ever had are with very wealthy guests. We've had more damage and deep clean-ups after these "elite" have stayed, and we've experienced the sense of entitlement from these guests. If you have a guest that is paying a higher rate, you should offer a premium service, but don't let yourself get taken advantage of. I now understand why there was a French Revolution.

People will sometimes ask for you to waive or to discount the cleaning fee when negotiating. They will also ask if they can do some of the cleaning themselves to receive a discount. My advice is to never ever discount the cleaning fee, and never ever leave any of the cleaning to be done by the guests. You will ask the guests to do a few items before they leave anyway, such as taking out the trash, making sure all dishes are done and starting a load of towels, but don't be lured in by the siren song of their good work ethic. Kelly's experiences as owner/

operator of a cleaning business confirms this point. As an added service to a property owner, she would double check a property after her cleaners were done, and in one case it was the property owner's in-laws that stayed there. They claimed they would clean up after themselves. Kelly ended up having to do a full-blown cleaning! She had to do it because guests just do not know how to clean like a professional does. Do not ever ask your cleaning person to ever discount their rate unless you want a discounted cleaning job. My response to guests who ask about discounting our cleaning rate or doing it themselves is that our cleaning fees and policy are non-negotiable. We like to treat our cleaning team as good as possible because our guests deserve the most pleasant and clean experience possible. I never have anyone argue that point with me.

Don't let this hard policy talk get you down. I told you in the beginning I was going to be honest with you because we all learned it the hard way, and I want you to have an edge. The truth is, the number of great guests and friends you will make in this business will far outnumber the issues that you have. Operating a vacation rental is rewarding because you get a chance to do business with some sincere people whose lives you will have the opportunity to effect in a positive and fulfilling way. Here is a real email that Kelly received from a guest at our first nightly rental property. This one forever stuck with me and reminds me that this business is about refreshing people. The money is just a bonus.

"Hello, Kelly! I wanted to let you know that we had a wonderful stay at The Quiet Cottage. After we planned this trip in August, my sister's husband passed away suddenly. At the age of 30, this is the last thing we thought we would be dealing with this holiday. We decided to go ahead with our plans since it was something that my brother-in-law was really looking forward to. Our time at your house was the perfect answer for a very difficult Christmas. It was peaceful, relaxing, and we enjoyed every moment there. Our children loved our 'Christmas House.' We're all thankful that Santa found our forwarding address, and the kids asked when we can go back.

Anyway, I just wanted to let you know that we enjoyed the home and what a difference our time there made. I hope you and your family had a nice holiday. - Jennifer K."

Inquiries

If people are contacting you, you are doing something right. They have questions, and it is your job to tackle them. The amount of inquiries you get is a test of how well your pictures, text and pricing are working for you. If you are not getting any inquiries, then it is probably one of these three things. Likewise, if you are getting too many inquiries and you cannot respond to all of them the same day, then you may want to increase your price to help slow them down. This means your property is in demand, and you have an opportunity to increase your rate.

The time and manner in which you respond to the inquiries will make you or break you. The best thing you can do is to respond to an inquiry right away. I bought my first smartphone so I could get access to my email for this reason alone. If you can prove that you are available now, it will prove that you will be available if something needs your attention while the guests are at the property. If you can't respond right away, you should at least respond by the end of the day. If you don't, they will most likely book with someone else who responded quicker. You are selling yourself as much as your property, so don't be afraid to put a little personality in your reply to them as I mentioned previously. Don't just offer the rate they asked for; tell them it is a beautiful day at your property. Tell them about the silly squirrel who keeps coming by to steal the bird food. Show them you are a real person. In your email back to them always ask this question: can you tell me a little bit about your group? This is paramount because it does two things for you. First, it will give you some information to help you determine if you want to rent to them or not. I don't have anything against strippers, but a group of frat guys can work your property over pretty good. On the other hand, a family coming down to celebrate Mom and Dad's 60th is probably a good bet. This is information you need to know before you tell them your property is available. Second, this question turns the table on the negotiations. It subtly tells the guest that they now need to sell themselves to you rather than you having to sell your property to them. If they have contacted you, then your property was selected above some others, and this is a good sign. Be polite, confident and friendly. Some of the websites will not offer you a chance to speak to your guest by phone, and some have automatic replies. You should attempt to respond personally. In our travel experience, we choose properties whose owners respond personally. We know if anything goes wrong or if we have any questions, they won't be too busy to get back with us. Asking this question gives you a chance to learn whatever you can about your guest.

You will get questions from time to time on giving discounts for AAA, Seniors or Military. This is up to you. We always offer one low rate for everyone, and when asked, we simply say we are not the (insert large hotel chain), and we are not holding anything back from our guests. We offer one low rate for everyone, and we hope you appreciate that policy. This usually goes over well because it honors all people equally. The men and women of the military deserve honor and discounts for their sacrifice. Seniors deserve discounts for their wisdom, contribution and fixed income status. AAA members deserve discounts because they had the forethought to join a club. Where do you stop? If people are used to getting a discount, they may want it from you. You will decide what works best for your property and personality.

Reviews

Your reviews will weigh heavy on your prospective guests' decision on whether or not to rent your home. If your property is good enough for the Joneses, it will be good enough for them. If you have enough great reviews, you won't have to sell yourself or the property at all because your past guests will do if for you. If you have done your job well, those reviews will even name you and say how great you were to work with. You can now see why selling yourself as well as your property is an important part of the plan. So, how do you get reviews? Ask for them. Once the guest has left, follow up with a very nice email thanking them for choosing you, and let them know they are welcome back any time. In this email, provide a link back to your site or to the review input site. Some of the websites that you use to advertise your property will allow you to set this up automatically. Another way to get reviews in the beginning is to offer to send them a five-dollar gift card to a coffee shop as a way of saying thank you for taking the time to post some comments. Once you get a few raving reviews, you won't have to offer incentives.

You should also leave a guestbook in your property. Guests will leave some wonderful comments for you, and it will help connect them to the property. Some sites let you manually enter these reviews into the review section. This way you can double up on your guest feedback a bit faster.

Guest reviews are a good way to hold you accountable, and they also hold other property owners accountable. If you give excellent service and maintain your property well, it will show in the reviews, and that's great because everyone deserves to know how great you are to work with.

Other deals, partnerships and promotions

Once you have mastered your pictures, marketing text, pricing, fielding inquiries and reviews, you can start to add some creativity. Now is when you should start reaching out to other property owners and offer them a referral fee for their overflow. Connecting with other owners can be a great way to catch some extra business. You can also contact hotels and see if they have a policy for overflow or double bookings. You might contact some local restaurants or attractions and offer to put their printed material or coupons in your home for a discount for your guests or perhaps for placing your property business cards in their establishment. Another great promotion that I've seen used successfully is to reach out to church or reunion groups and offer to put them in a drawing for a free week rental. This is especially beneficial to do during the off season because it allows your home some well-deserved activity, plus it doesn't take away income-producing weekends during the peak season. Once you've built your contact database of churches or reunion groups, pull out a name, and let everyone on the list know who the winner is. Honor your agreement, and now you will have a great contact list to market to. In one case where this was successful, the winning church group used the home for a pastor retreat. The pastor came back so thankful and so refreshed, he couldn't stop talking about the place. The next thing you know, the whole congregation was booking up the home. The options are unlimited when you begin to think about it, and you are allowed to go as crazy as you want to, but not until your website is in tip top shape, you are excellent at fielding inquiries and you understand that reviews can make your life easier.

Receiving the money

Money in the bank is the result of your great marketing strategy. How much you decide to take as a deposit will be up to you and the market that you are working in. When I say deposit, I mean half of the entire total. Here is what the deposit amount will look like: RENT + TAX + DAMAGE DEPOSIT + CLEANING FEE x ½ = DEPOSIT

A successful strategy is to take half down at the time of booking and the remaining amount is due thirty to sixty days prior to their arrival, according to the terms of your rental agreement. If the dates they are booking is less than thirty to sixty days away, then the total is due immediately. Your cancellation policy will need to be defined here, as well. We will talk about that a bit later.

When the guest pays the remaining amount due and rent is paid in full, this is when you deliver the access code/key code and directions to your property. You don't have to mail keys or personal checks anymore. You can easily apply for a merchant account or use one of the many software programs available. These programs completely automate the booking and money transfer process. The money goes directly into an account that you've created specifically for this property so you can track its individual success.

Chapter Six

Nine Rules You Should Never Break When Operating a Nightly Rental

Once you are set up, getting inquiries and you understand the importance of reviews, it's time to start thinking about your operation. This part is easier than riding a bike, and you'll have far fewer skinned knees. The best part about operating a vacation rental is that your guests are really good at going on vacation. At this point, they have probably done this more times than you. They know how it works, and it takes a lot to screw this part up. You've taken the inquiry, collected some money, given the code to the property, so now it's your property's job to do the rest. If you have done a thorough job with your setup and are a good communicator with your guests, the property will do a wonderful job. Here are some tried and true tips to make things run even smoother for you.

Put directions and your phone number on your rental agreement

Your rental agreement is your first chance to do some real business with your prospective guest, and it will give them a chance to see your rules and regulations. If you can't agree at this point, it's probably not a good fit, although it usually goes smoothly. Even if you subscribe to an automated website service where the guest will review an uploaded copy of your agreement and "sign off" on it by booking your property, it is still a great idea to email them a separate attachment of your rules, regulations, directions and contact information. There are still many old-school folks who like to print things out. This way you can be sure to highlight some of your more important rules.

Put any very pertinent information in the first paragraph of the rental agreement. Next, put your dates and firm check-in and check-out times. Then add your directions and your phone number, followed by the rest of your agreement. Don't bury important information into the body because most guests don't even read the whole thing. Be sure to have a guest count in your agreement; otherwise they might be tempted to load up on extra family. Too many people in your home may be against municipal fire codes and just doesn't help with wear and tear on the property. Don't plan on them reading the rules if your vacation rental is in a development; be sure to state them in your rental agreement and print off a copy for them to read at the home. Finally, if you send an agreement as an attachment in an e-mail, using the body of the e-mail to highlight important items is a good idea. Here is an example:

> *Hi, Sandy!*
> *We hope you are looking forward to your stay at The Quiet Cottage! As a reminder, check-in is after 4 p.m. on June 1, and check-out is before 10 a.m. on June 5. The code to the door is 1234. For your convenience, I am attaching the rental agreement/license to stay agreement which will have directions, contact information, and our rules. We hope you have a wonderful stay!*
>
> *Jeramie & Kelly*

Have a firm cancellation policy

Having a firm cancellation policy is important because it will happen to you. Knowing how to handle this before it happens will make you seem more professional and will give you more control of the situation.

I understand death in the family, and I'm sympathetic, but sometimes it's an obvious farce. It never fails that one of the family members cancels, and the rest of the group has to bear the additional burden of per-night cost. Uncle Derek never dies three to four months in advance; he always seems to die about two weeks before your guests are supposed to arrive. Your firm stance on the policy will show the guest that they are dealing with a professional and will help weed out the circus tricks.

Here are two ways to handle the situation that will help you have compassion without missing out on the rental revenue it if they are already past their cancellation window. Tell them you are very sorry and choose one of the following responses:

1. Tell them you will open the dates and give them a refund for whatever days book up.
2. Keep their money and offer them a credit for a future stay.

If they ask what your cancellation policy is before they book your home, that could be a red flag. Read them the policy from your agreement, and then ask them if they anticipate needing to cancel. They will then tell you what is on their mind: possible weather problems or someone in the family is sick. You can direct them to go ahead and get cancellation insurance for a small fee that will be well worth it. We did have guests who were concerned about a family member not making it through the holidays. The week before their reservation, the family member passed away, and they had to cancel. The woman who made the reservation had to jump through a few hoops to get her money back, including having me talk directly to the insurance company, but in the end, she got her money back. It was beneficial for her and for us in that there was not enough time to get another renter in at such late notice, and she got her full amount back.

Take a damage deposit

If you don't take a damage deposit, eventually you'll change your mind. The amount will change based on the size and location of your property and the amenities you offer, but a good average number is about $300. When we started, we would hold a check and mail it back if no damages were found. Now, we go ahead and charge the deposit, and our marketing website automatically refunds it seven days after their departure if no damages are found. Your rental agreement will spell out what your expectations are. Some owners even charge a fee if you are late checking out. I've seen some agreements that charge you by the minute! A great feature offered by many websites is a damage insurance, so be sure to check on that because it can be a good idea.

So what happens if you find some damage? The first question to ask is: is this the hill I want to die on? If you are continually frustrated by missing washcloths, then just don't get into this business. There will be minor things that happen, and you don't need to call your guest on each one of them. Chalk it up to the cost of doing business, and be sure to get a great review out of the guest. The long list of great reviews is worth the cost of a few minor things. When something does break or go missing, don't be afraid to question your guest about it. They may not even know. It could have been another family member who did it and just kept things quiet. One time, Kelly was cleaning a property with very expensive handmade quilts. Because she cleaned the property four to five times a month, she knew immediately one was missing. She let the owner she was working for know, and a call was made to the guest. The guest was flabbergasted, and after some investigation found out that Aunt Beth had taken the quilts! They were promptly mailed back and no damages assessed.

Don't worry so much about damage; it does happen, but in the many years we've been at this, we've only had to charge people twice. The first time, I already mentioned about the Wii remote in the TV, and the other time we had an unauthorized pet in a property with an unforgiving bladder. So we had the carpets cleaned and charged $150 to the guest, and all was good.

Have a check-in and check-out note

If you want to wow your guest even more, leave a small gift basket for them with a welcome note. Something small like a box of chocolates or some popcorn and candy always goes over well. Choose something you can easily stock up on and keep in your locked owner's closet for the cleaning person to set out after the place is clean. Your check-in note should make them feel welcome and give them helpful information, such as how to get into a community amenity, some basic parking rules, where to find an extra tank of propane for the gas grill, how to change the input on the TV to get from cable to the DVD player, what the Wi-Fi password is, where to put their bags of trash, etc. This part should highlight the simple tips for your guest that should make your life easier. You'll know what to put in this note because it will be the four to five questions you get all of the time. The note will save you a lot of phone time and will help you stop potential problems before they arise. Chances are you will change this note over time with the most common situations you are dealing with. We keep our note on the refrigerator and keep extras in the owner's closet in case it gets tossed or starts to look worn.

The following is a sample check-in note:

Welcome to The Cozy Condo!

Thank you for choosing our home away from home for your vacation. We hope you will find your stay comfortable and enjoyable.

Just a reminder that your check-out time is by 10 a.m. Please keep in mind we will have a cleaning crew coming at that time. Upon check out, we would very much appreciate some help out with the following:

1. All debris, rubbish and discards are placed in dumpster, and soiled dishes are placed in the dishwasher and cleaned. Dumpster is located just down the stairs and to the right inside the fenced area.

2. Dirty linens are placed in laundry room and one load of towels is started.

3. Sheets and pillowcases are taken off the beds (please leave mattress protectors and pillow protectors unless they need to be washed.

4. Keys are placed back in the lockbox and unit is left locked.

The Wi-Fi username is: **Suddenlink.netF16**
Pass phrase is: **WElcomE!**

To operate the TV in the living room:

- Use the TV remote to turn the TV on or off or to manage the volume.

- Use the SuddenLink remote to operate the cable. Press the "Cable" button on the top of the remote and then press "Power" to turn the cable on. Then you can navigate the cable with the same SuddenLink remote.

- To watch a DVD, use the input button on the TV remote and continue to press the input button until the "AV" picture is highlighted. Then turn the power on the DVD player, and you are in business.

- To go back to TV mode, use the input button on the TV remote and continue to press the button until the "HDMI" picture is highlighted. You are ready to watch the cable with the SuddenLink remote now (see bulletpoint 2 above)!

If you have any questions or problems during your stay, please call us at _____. We are happy to help.

Enjoy your time,
Kelly & Jeramie

To give you an example of how powerful a check-in note can be, the following is an example of a note that Kelly and I used in one of our properties in the summer time. During the peak of the summer, the temperatures would stay above one hundred, and we started to get calls from our guests that the property was too hot in the evening. The air conditioner would not keep up at all. We called an HVAC professional (Heating Ventilation and Air Conditioning), and he said that you can only get about a twenty-degree variance from the exterior temperature out of your unit in the summer. So, if it was a hundred degrees outside, the temperature inside would only be as cool as eighty. We tinted the windows on the west side of the house and provided some nice fans for every room, and we still kept getting calls. One summer afternoon, we drove by the property around check-in time, and we noticed the guests had left the front door wide open as they were loading in. At a 3-4 p.m. check-in time, hot air is an unwelcome guest in the summer, and, if left unattended, it will sneak right in. We modified our check-in note with the following language, and our calls went from all the time to almost zero.

TIPS TO STAY COOL THIS SUMMER
For your comfort, we have tinted the windows on the west side of the home. We have also provided extra fans upstairs and have the air conditioner regularly serviced by a professional. Here are some things you can do to keep yourselves cool:

1. Keep the front door closed at all times (especially upon load in and load out)

2. Keep the thermostat set on 71. Do not adjust it to the lowest setting. Doing so could freeze up the unit, leaving you without any air conditioning at all.
3. If you would like, close a few air vents in the lower level at night to force cooler air upstairs.

Don't look overlook this check-in/check-out note; it can be a real life saver, and it is another opportunity to help your guest have a comfortable stay. Likewise, your check-out checklist is just as helpful. Your check-out checklist can be on the same note as the check-in information or you can provide a separate note. The check-out instructions will serve two purposes. One, it will help hold your guests accountable because they know they will be partially responsible for their own cleanup of certain items, although you don't want to go overboard here. Two, you will be asking them to do just enough to give your cleaning staff a head start.

If you go overboard with your check-out checklist, it can negatively affect your reviews. After all, your guests are paying a cleaning fee, so they will want to see some value from that. We've found that if you keep it simple, guests are happy to help out.

Handle issues right away

Issues can be the best thing that ever happened to you because it gives you the opportunity to get an amazing review. Travelers understand that things happen, but it's how you handle those things that make you shine. Be sure you have a list of numbers for a handyman, appliance repair, HVAC person, utility company and homeowners association, as these are the most common major issues.

We once received a note at the property from a group of guests who had experienced a power outage while visiting our nightly rental. They told us that since we did not have flashlights or candles at the house, they went and bought some and left them there for future guests. While they were out, they also bought a rug to put at the back door and a small table lamp to go on the side of a bed. They also recommended a universal remote for the living room as well as a full-length mirror so guests could see their entire outfit before going out to shows or dinner. We could have been offended at the suggestions, but instead, we sent the guests a gift certificate for a meal and thanked them for the helpful suggestions. We took those suggestions and added a mirror and a universal remote control.

Handle issues fast. Things are going to happen. As long as you handle it fast, that's what counts. Here is another real-life example. One time we had a brand new refrigerator go out. It was only thirteen months-old and just one month out of the factory warranty. When

I received the call from the guest about the sluggish machine, I sent out the repairman who let me know it was a Freon line leak and that I'd have to call the manufacturer to work out a replacement claim. I wasn't about to make the guests suffer without a refrigerator while I hashed out my differences with the corporate office, so I called the big box store where I purchased the appliance, explained the situation and they had a new fridge delivered the same day. They even hauled off the old one and kept it for me until I could resolve the claim. As you grow your nightly rental enterprise, you'll have more and better contacts on your power team that help make your life easier.

Consider your pet policy carefully

I love my pooch, and I love your pooch, but many of the prospective renters who are looking at your property may not love either of ours. We've done it both ways. We accepted pets, and we did get a great deal of business because of it. If you do this, then be sure you have an additional pet addendum to your rental agreement. You will want to charge an extra fee per night, and be sure to place a limit on pets (we learned this one the hard way). If you do accept pets, say you are "pet friendly" but that you consider them on a case by case basis. This still gives you an out if your guests have any giraffe-sized dogs. If you accept pets, you run the risk of becoming pet central. That is what happened to us. We made more money for it, and all we had to do was clean the carpets an extra time per year and add an additional amount to the cleaning for the extra time it took to clean up dog hair.

The major downside to accepting pets is that many people who are sensitive to animals or have allergies will pass on your property because you do accept pets. If you do not accept pets and you advertise that you do not, your property may appeal to those folks are looking for a very clean place to stay. Either way works; these are just a few points to consider before making your final decision.

Watch out for scammers

It doesn't happen frequently that you will get scam emails, but when you do, they are pretty obvious. It is usually the same old story about a person who wants to send a cashier's check for the full amount. The emails are usually full of grammatical errors, but I have seen people fall for them. If you are unsure about an inquiry, it is best to just not respond to it. If it feels normal, it probably is. If the questions about the property and terms of business feel like all of the other transactions you've done, it's probably ok. I wouldn't go out of your way to accommodate a payment request for a stranger. Be in control of your property and the way you do business, and you will avoid the scammer pitfall. If you are still unsure, run it by a friend or colleague. Sometimes your eagerness to rent a property, especially in the early days, can inhibit your ability think logically, so running it by a second set of eyes can help keep you smart. I've talked to many owners who think it is a good practice to google a person's name or to look them up on Facebook before you rent to them. The extra information can't hurt.

Keep an extra hidden key handy

This commonly overlooked practice will save your bacon. If you ever have a problem with your electronic code or if your renter ever loses their key, this will help you solve an immediate and urgent need with an easy one-step, especially if you are managing your nightly rental from another city or state. I like to call this the contractor key. It's a good idea to have a contractor key handy if there is an issue and you need to get a repairman into the property while the guest is out enjoying their vacation. The guest will need to take their key, so be sure to have another one hidden in a coded lockbox nearby. We typically leave a hidden key in the nightly rental that goes to the owner's closet, as well, which will be used by the cleaning person to access all of the cleaning supplies.

Don't say you are handicapped accessible if you are not

Be accommodating but be smart. Unless you have had your property inspected by someone who is familiar with all of the ADA (Americans with Disabilities Act) rules and regulations, I would not advertise your property as "handicapped accessible." This is a term that is reserved for properties that have taken special care to make sure they have added wider doorways, ramps, lower counters, reinforced handles near toilets and showers and a long list of other requirements. If your property is a walk-in home, simply say that it is a walk-in home and has no stairs. Describe the property, not who you think the property would be good for, and you'll avoid getting into trouble. If someone calls and asks if the property is "handicapped accessible," be honest. Tell them that the property does not have any stairs and can be accessed by a wheelchair, but that it is not an official handicapped accessible property and that if they have any concern whatsoever, you are happy to help further describe your property.

Chapter Seven

Exit Strategy

Why on earth would you want to sell your top-performing vacation rental? It happens. Life changes for people. Some people sell a two-bedroom to upgrade to a four-bedroom. Some found a new place they wanted to vacation, and some just move on with life. When my grandpa rounded eighty years old, he started wondering if there would be anything left for Grandma should anything happen to him. Because of the rules that surrounded his pension, she would get nothing if he went to meet the Good Lord first. His motive was having his assets liquid. That's what he told me, but I know for a fact he's been to the Mini Cooper lot at least seven times since he's gotten his dirty little hands on that cash. I thought I'd catch him busting out of the car lot in that Mini Cooper, all Jesse Pinkman style, but alas, he did save the money for Grandma. He's a man of his word. After we sold the property, he did get hit by the capital gains bus, and his tax shelter went up in smoke. His tax liability went back up, so I told him it was ok for him to start complaining about the government again. Whatever the reason, someday you may need to sell.

When you start to get the word out, every single prospective buyer will ask why the property is for sale. Nosy colleagues will want your income numbers for a free look, so it helps to have a strategy in place before you put that sign out. In some upscale resort communities, real estate signs are prohibited. You'll need some help. To sell it right means to sell it for the right price and to ethically do the right thing. It helps to have a well laid out plan before you put the property on the market.

What to look for in a selling agent

Just because a real estate agent sells a lot of properties in the community does not necessarily mean they are a good agent. I know plenty of agents who know what a property will sell for, but they have no idea what price a nightly rental property could actually bring. Experience is the first thing you are looking for. You want to find someone who has sold many nightly rentals before and knows how to handle everything that goes with it. Since you are selling a money machine and not just a piece of real estate, you need an agent that regularly sells money machines. This is not to say you need to go out and get a commercial real estate agent, but a residential agent who has experience selling vacation rentals should be the next trait you are looking for. This way they will be able to help you understand the value of your home with and without bookings and understand the seasonal aspect of the business. Sales comparisons and active listings of other vacation rentals will give you a good start, but you also need to compare the income your property generates to the income of similar properties to get a true picture of the value of your property. Optimism is the next thing that you are looking for. It is nice to be in business with someone who believes they can succeed. You want to be sure that you will get as much value as you can out of the property, the furniture and the potential bookings. The third thing you will need to know about your agent is if they have a strong contact database of other vacation rental owners. If so, they will be able to market your property privately, and this will help you continue to book the property while the unit is for sale.

Here is a list of interview questions to ask your prospective real estate agent:

1. Have you ever sold a vacation rental before?
2. How do you price a home that includes furniture and bookings?
3. What is the best time to list a vacation rental home?
4. What are the comparable properties selling for?
5. What is the average time on the market for a nightly rental?
6. What do you recommend that I do with personal items or personal property that I want to keep and not sell with the property?
7. Do I have to list my home on the MLS?
8. If I don't want to list my home on the MLS, what avenues can you use to market or sell my property?
9. Do I need to sell contact lists and websites that go along with the property?
10. Should I put the property in an LLC and sell it or just sell the property?

Make sure they know the value

Price per square foot is the worst determining factor of value for a vacation rental. When you buy a luxury item, you don't buy by the increment. You don't buy a Mercedes by the price per square inch; you buy it because it's a Mercedes. It has four wheels, windows and a radio, but it is so much more than just transportation. There is something about it that makes it better. Selling a vacation rental is the same because your home will have some special feature, such as a lake view, walking distance to a clubhouse or pool, privacy or a custom outdoor kitchen. This will give a subjective value to the property. You need an agent who can help you price these values in addition to the functional factors, such as bedrooms and living space.

Experience can guide you through a Smoother Transition

Having an agent with experience selling vacation rentals will help tremendously because they can help you navigate the transfer and disposition of the bookings. Your bookings are incredibly valuable to you because they add real cash value to your property, and they are enticing to a new buyer because they are buying an active business. The buyer might get a check at closing for the rent you have collected, and who wouldn't want to start this way? It's like buying a restaurant with customers already in the store eating pancakes. When they came in, the restaurant was owned by someone else, but they pay you on the way out.

When you do transfer the bookings, the most important thing is to keep the guests in mind when you sell your property. These are people who could have chosen to stay in a hotel. They could have chosen another property for their family vacation, but they didn't. They chose you, and it is your job to make sure they are taken care of when you sell. You may not want to reveal to the guest that you are selling the property. I know this seems contradictory my statements of ethics, but it's not. This is a very common practice with the sale of a business so that service to the guest is not interrupted.

You've already made sure that their rental contracts will be honored per your sales contract, you've made sure the new owner of the property has all of the contact information for the incoming guests and vice versa, so all you need to do now is make sure that there is a warm hand-off to the new property manager. Telling them that you are selling the property could cause them to freak out unnecessarily and cancel. This could be bad for you and the new owner. Nothing will change. The new owner is now the new "property manager," and they are stepping in for you. You will introduce the new owner in an email and mention that this is the person they should contact moving forward. Here is a sample email.

Dear Janet,

This is just a quick courtesy note to, once again, confirm your reservation at The Lucky Day Lodge for July 2-4. I wanted to let you know that the home has a new property manager, so if you have any questions, feel free to contact John Homebuyer at email@email.com or (555) 555-1234. I am always happy to help you, but I wanted to introduce John who will be collecting the balance of your rent and aiding if you need anything upon your arrival.

Best Regards,
Alice Seller

This practice ensures good communication with the guest and the new property owner. Next, it is the buyer's job to follow up with an introductory email.

Good morning, Janet!

I'm emailing to introduce myself as the new property manager for The Lucky Day Lodge. I know that Alice wrote to you to give you my contact information, but I wanted to take a moment to introduce myself personally. We are looking forward to your stay.

Best,
John Homebuyer

If you go into the dry cleaner's, they are not going to tell you they sold the property to new people. You just need your clothes cleaned and ironed, and as long as you are getting that service, you are a happy customer. Feel good about it, and feel good about the sale. If you want to feel rewarded for your work you have already done booking the property, try to negotiate a booking fee for yourself in the sales contract. You heard me! Don't just give your bookings away with your property. Charge the new buyer a booking fee of ten to fifteen percent if you intended to let them manage the new bookings or twenty to thirty percent if you intend to manage your bookings for the new owner until they take over. This booking fee will be deducted from the total rent that you owe the new buyer at closing.

Be Careful if you list the property on the MLS

Most of the websites where home buyers begin their search for new properties are populated with data that is pulled from an IDX (Internet Data Exchange) feed that comes directly from local and regional MLS (Multiple Listing Service) organizations. When your property is listed, within twenty hours it goes out to potentially 300 syndicate websites. This could be detrimental to you because when your future guest plugs your address into google, it will come up "FOR SALE" and, trust me, you'll get a call. There are a few scams out there of people posing as vacation rental owners attempting to collect money from vacationers, and the savvy traveler will be looking you up.

Sell the property furnished

If you can offer a turnkey rental, you will stand out, especially if you are selling the property in a development with new construction. If a prospective buyer can choose your fully-furnished property for a price similar to new construction, more often than not, they will choose the turnkey property. You are not going to get full retail value for your used furniture, so don't bother trying. If you use this strategy, you may be considered overpriced, and you can miss out on prospective buyers.

Sell like a boss

Prepare a pro forma for the property and back it up with the past two years' schedule E from your tax return. Don't create a word document; that's what everyone else does, and it's easily manipulated. Don't give these out to anyone who asks but wait for people who show a very strong interest in the property. Be sure to black out any social security numbers or information for other properties. Use caution but don't be a scrooge with the information. How can a buyer determine the value for the property and make an offer if they have no idea what it brings? If you are concerned with privacy, have the buyer sign a non-disclosure statement. You need to be prepared with this information prior to selling your home because it will help you stand out as organized and professional.

Here are some other strategies you can use

• **Put some marketing material inside the home to sell to renters.** You'd be surprised who goes on vacation and ends up coming home with a $400,000 souvenir.
• **Sell the home to a past renter.** You have a database of hundreds of inquiries and past customers. Don't feel bad about sending out a special note about your home.
• **Reserve some items for yourself.** If you plan to buy another home, keep back just enough items to make it easy for yourself and that won't be a large enough miss for the buyer to really notice. Of course you'll want to disclose these items at the time of the offer, but something like: extra linens, paper products, tools and a gas grill. This will save you some bucks because you'll need them, and a new buyer can easily go out and get those.
• **Rent the property back until your bookings are done.** If you are dead set on getting all the value out of your bookings and the new owner will not be renting out or using the home, you can always lease the property from the new owners until you are done with your business. Grandpa and I did this with our first sale because we sold it just two months before the off season. We negotiated this lease back as a way to maximize our income out of

the property before we let it go.

• **List your home on commercial websites.** A couple of good ones to mention are www.loopnet.com and www.bizbuysell.com. These websites have worked for us in the past to generate leads from savvy business owners looking for a good rate of return.

• **Don't wait until the off season to sell your property.** This is the best piece of advice you can get in regard to selling your vacation rental. Waiting until the off season is what everyone else does, and when inventory goes up, competition goes up and prices go down. Sell when you need to sell, but consider incentivizing your buyer with some good bookings. You want to salt that juicy meat. Trust me…it works.

Chapter Eight
Benefits, Rules & the IRS
with Richard Carraway, CPA

DISCLAIMER

Any accounting, business or tax advice contained in this chapter is not intended as a thorough, in-depth analysis of specific issues, nor a substitute for a formal opinion, nor is it sufficient to avoid tax-related penalties. Please consult with a certified public accountant and/or attorney for advice for your specific situation.

I was asked by my friend, Jeramie, to write a chapter from the perspective of a CPA and active investor in nightly rentals. He mentioned that he was tired of reading advice from people who had to disclaim that they were not a CPA. We all know that talking about tax laws can get tedious and difficult to understand, but I am going to do my best to put this into layman's terms so that you feel more fully educated on the ins and outs of the nightly rental industry. Jeramie also mentioned that it was important for this book that the CPA could speak from experience as a real estate investor. I am Richard Carraway, and I'm both. I am the managing partner of my firm. I am a practicing CPA, and so is my wife, Jessica. I'm the one writing this chapter, but she's the one reading over my shoulder making sure I don't leave anything out. We want to make sure you get great information to help you run your business. Even though we may not be your CPAs, there are some general rules that you can follow to maximize your benefits.

When I rolled into town twenty years ago, I had nothing but the shirt on my back, a nine-year-old Cutlass Supreme and a hunger like a chicken eating ticks. I borrowed $1,000 against that car to put a deposit down to rent my first apartment. While I don't have that car anymore, I still have the hunger for a better life, thus my love for investing. We currently own six vacation rentals, which we actively manage. We discovered the potential of nightly rentals through the power of numbers, which is our forte. We were able to back up our estimated first year rates of return with "live" numbers generated by a friend actively working in the market where we wanted to buy. While much of this chapter is to help you select the best CPA for your team, our first recommendation is to find a real estate agent with experience in this field. It will pay dividends. We were actually able to speak with some of Jeramie's clients before we jumped in with both feet. We closed on five of our properties within a thirty-day period, which worked out well in the end, but we would not recommend this. In addition to operating a full-time accounting practice, we are also raising three children, and two of them were under three years old at the time. If we can do that, you can get started on your first property. Here is what you need to know.

Getting Started

In addition to finding a realtor who knows the business, I would strongly encourage you to engage all of the following professionals in order to ensure your success: accountant, attorney, banker, 1031 intermediary and insurance agent. These are the people that can get you started on the right track and guide you through the process. It is my experience that if you don't have the right people, you will find out some things the hard way. For example, I am a CPA practicing in Arkansas, so I didn't know the sales tax rules for Missouri where I purchased my investment properties. One of the landlords I talked to told me that all of the sales tax is due after year end. I took that to heart and did not file my first year's sales tax until the following January. That's when I found out that part should have been filed quarterly and part monthly, thus I was rewarded with penalties for late filing and payment. Talk to the professionals for advice, not people on the street.

Budgeting

As you get started, get with your CPA, realtor and/ or other investors, and prepare a realistic budget of expenses. Be sure and make an effort to include every expense that you may incur. Once this list of expenses is complete, divide it by the number of days that you realistically expect to rent the property. That will give you an important number. That number is the nightly rental rate you would charge to break even. It is an aid to help determine the minimum price that you need to advertise your property. For our properties, we divide by 100 days for the maximum pricing and 150 days for average pricing to get a conservative range. Then, we do an average between the two. If you rent your property too cheap, you will not make money and you may not even cover your costs.

Here is an example of the formula we use to position ourselves for success:

Total Annual Expenses divided by 100 = maximum per night rate

$14,000.00 in Total Annual Expenses / 100 = $140.00 maximum price per night

Total Annual Expenses divided by 150 = average price purchase price

$14,000.00 in Total Annual Expenses / 150 = $93.33 minimum price per night

We know we will rent the property for more than 100 nights, and most cases we do more than 150, but at least we have a baseline and know that we should never discount our rate below $93.33 per night. Measure that against the market and avoid discounting your price line below this average.

Record keeping

It is imperative that you keep good records of income and expenses as well as the time that you spend taking care of your rental business. The time records are important in determining the deductions you may be able to take. The key phrase the IRS uses is "material participation." This is a highly important topic we will discuss in just a moment. It is strongly recommended that you maintain a separate bank account for your rental activities. A separate bank account is required if you hold your rental properties inside of a separate legal entity, such as an LLC. Once again, your CPA can help you set up your books before you begin, rather than try to piece together the information after the fact. You should keep a record of each rental and all expenses that you incur. Bear in mind, cancelled checks do not constitute proof of an expense. You need to keep all receipts and invoices for any expenses paid. If you pay by credit or debit card, staple the receipts to the statement each month. Indicate on the receipt what the expense was for, and if you have multiple properties, indicate which property it is for. We use QuickBooks for our record keeping and have set up classes so that we can keep each property's income and expenses separate. The IRS will allow a one-time election to combine all of your properties into one or you will have to report each property separately. We usually recommend that you use separate reporting to help determine the success of each property.

Types of rental properties

With respect to rental property, there are three basic tax situations for second homes:

1. You rent the property to others most or all of the year (investment).
2. You use the property yourself and rent it when you are not using it (vacation home).
3. You only rent the property a few days a year (2nd home, not a rental).

If you fall into the first category, then you rarely, if ever, use the property for personal use. If you use it less than fourteen days per year, then it is not considered a home, but an investment property. If you have no personal use, you can deduct all expenses against the income received. If you use the property for personal use for more than fourteen days per year, it becomes a vacation home/investment property, and expenses have to be prorated based on days used. Finally, if you rent your second home out for less than fourteen days per year total, you do not report the income at all, and you do not deduct your expenses. You still may deduct mortgage interest and property taxes on Schedule A of Form 1040 (if you can itemize). For more in-depth details, see IRS Publication 527.

Income

What is included in income? For starters, the direct rental income generated by the property is considered income. Other items can be considered income, including pet fees, booking fees, damage charges, referral fees received and even cleaning fees collected. Sales tax is not income. *I repeat, sales tax is not income. It is not your money; it is a liability that must be calculated, collected and remitted to the proper agencies.* Cleaning fees, on the other hand, are income, whether or not you clean your own property or if you pay someone else to clean it. Cleaning fees paid to others are an offsetting expense that you can deduct later.

Deductions

What are allowable deductions? Here are a few examples:

Accounting	Advertising
Bank Charges	Cleaning Fees
Computer Expenses	Credit Card Fees
Depreciation	HOA/COA Dues
Insurance	Interest
Linens	Meals
Office Expenses	Pest Control
Legal Fees	Repairs & Maintenance
Supplies	Occupation Licenses
Telephone	Electric
Water	Sewer
Cable/Satellite	Internet
Trash Collection	Travel
Property Taxes	Mileage

For 2015, you may be entitled to deduct 57.5 cents per mile for all travel related to maintaining your rental property. Keep in mind that this mileage rate changes often. You may also be entitled to 50% off business meals, provided that you document the business purpose of the meal and the names of the other parties involved. This list is not intended to be an all-inclusive list but certainly a list that can be used in the budgeting process. Mortgage interest is largely beneficial because your renter is paying it, not you, yet you get to take the deduction at tax time. Additionally, do not forget that the renter is also paying the principle of the loan down each year, as well, and you get to keep that money. You don't see it on your bottom line, but it is there, it is yours and you can access it when you sell or refinance. Don't forget about that because it is all part of your annual rate of return.

Sales tax & licensing

Before you rent the first night, make sure that you have all of the proper licensing to do business, including collection of sales tax and any necessary bonding. Vacation Rentals are a hybrid of a traditional rental property and a commercial enterprise, and some states see them differently. More often than not, you will have to pay commercial taxes in your county, pay sales tax in your state and follow your local and state lodging laws, so you will want to be sure you are compliant. In many states, short-term rentals (less than 30 days), require the collection and remittance of sales tax. Often, long-term rentals (thirty days or more) are not subject to sales tax. In some states, counties and cities, there may be additional tourism taxes that must also be collected and remitted. It is important to know what constitutes taxable services, what the tax rates are, and when and where to file. Your CPA can help you with the proper licensing and filing of the required reports.

 TIP: EVEN IF YOU DO NOT COLLECT THE PROPER TAX, YOU ARE STILL RESPONSIBLE FOR REMITTING THE TAX.

You may also be subject to "use tax" in some states. Use tax is paid on items purchased tax-free from out of state, such as things ordered from Amazon. If you order your supplies online and are not taxed on them, you may be subject to use tax.

Like tourism tax, there may be some local rules you want to consider. First, you want to make sure the property you are buying is an approved vacation rental in the development and in your county. Some developments have restrictions on these types of properties, so do not overlook this important first step. You can usually discover this by talking to the planning and zoning department in the city or county that the property is located in. Furthermore, you will want to insure your property with a commercial policy that will provide you with enough adequate coverage, not only for liability, but also for loss of income due to your inability to use the property for major damages or natural disasters.

Passive Activity Rules and Material Participation

Passive Activity is a term the IRS uses to consider you a non-participating real estate investor. You may own the property but someone else is doing the management. It's funny (not really) that if the IRS considers your activity "passive," they can limit or disallow your losses. This is important because those losses are usually caused by all of the mortgage interest you are deducting. In general, rental activities will be defined by the IRS as passive activities. With passive activity, there are income limitations and a phase-out point in which your excess passive losses may be suspended or carried forward to future years. For those in high income brackets that have no other passive losses, these losses could be suspended until the passive activity is disposed of. So how do you dispose of passive activity? You have to roll up your sleeves and possibly get around the passive activity rules through material participation, which means you are taking an active role in operating your rental property. If you not materially participating in your property, then the IRS says that it is passive income, and you will only be able to deduct up to the amount of income you earn from the property. However, if you materially participate, then you will bypass the passive activity rules, and you will be able to take full advantage of all of your deductions and get into tax shelter territory. A tax shelter is created when deductions from an investment are greater than the income earned from the investment, and the difference starts to protect your ordinary income earned from a job or other business.

There are tests to determine whether or not you are actively participating, including determining the amount of time actually spent taking care of the management and/or maintenance of the rental property. Please see IRS Publication 925 Passive Activities and At-Risk Rules.

Depreciation

Depreciation is a beast. It is hard to understand. It's an ugly, hairy recluse that may as well be locked up in a library castle in the woods. Yet, when you begin to learn about it, it is tender and loving and misunderstood. When you master it, all the cupboards, cups and silverware come to life and perform musical numbers for your pleasure.

Residential rental property is depreciated under Modified Accelerated Cost Recovery System (MACRS) over a life of 27.5 years. Any land that may be acquired with the rental property must be accounted for separately and is not depreciable nor deductible. If you purchase a property that is fully furnished, you may allocate the purchase price between the real estate and the personal property, as long as the allocated values are within reason.

Personal property, acquired initially or after the date of purchase, is going to be depreciated under MACRS over five years. It is important to note the amount of the purchase price that you've allocated to the furniture and other personal property, such as appliances, electronics and the like. Personal property acquired at the time of purchase can accelerate the depreciation allowed in the first five years, reducing income subject to tax, which helps redirect tax dollars toward reduction of debt, return of equity or cash flow. The rules are complex, as is the record keeping; thus, we recommend that you consult your tax professional, preferably a CPA. Failure to follow the rules can have serious consequences.

Here is an example of how this works:

- The purchase price of a fully-furnished rental property is $300,000.
- $30,000 of that purchase price is allocated to furniture and appliances in the home.
- The personal property amount of $30,000 is divided by 5 years and equals a $6,000 deduction on first year's tax return, which results in a tax savings of $1,500 for a person in a 25% tax bracket.

Like-Kind Exchanges (Section 1031)

Deprecation is not entirely dreamy because there are some strict rules that go along with it but…only if you sell the property. There is no time frame for depreciation. If you sell the property, recapture applies, and the IRS can make you reclaim the deprecation if you've been taking it. So if you have plans to sell, you may not want to take a depreciation deduction. Be sure to talk to your tax manager or CPA about your situation. You may not ever have to sell your property, and if you do, you may consider "exchanging it" for a similar property. Look into a 1031 Like-Kind Exchange. Once rental property has been depreciated, the sale of this property can potentially generate a large tax liability. Often, a sale is going to result in ordinary income to recapture the depreciation taken. Why is this important? Only the amount of money you get at the sale that exceeds the original purchase cost is eligible for capital gains treatment. Capital gains are usually taxed at a lower rate than ordinary income. One way to postpone the tax consequence of selling your nightly rental is to trade real estate under Section 1031 of the Internal Revenue Code. The simplest type of 1031 Like-Kind Exchange is one property being traded for another like-kind property. You trade your condo for another condo of like value, and no gain or loss occurs. You can exchange money and boot. Boot is considered cash or other property added to an exchange in order to make the value of the traded goods equal. If there is money exchanged, or boot, then gain may be taxed up to the amount of boot received. The beautiful thing about real estate is that all real estate is like-kind. You can trade land for a building, an apartment for a condo, etc. The property must constitute real estate and must be within the United States. There are also special rules for deferred like-kind exchanges, where you sell your property using a qualified third-party intermediary and later replace the property with another like-kind property. There are strict rules with respect to the timing of acquiring replacement property that must be adhered to.

There is also the even more complex reverse exchange, also known as a Starker Exchange, where the replacement property is identified and purchased prior to the sale of the property to be "traded." Anyone who is interested in doing a Like-Kind Exchange should consult their tax advisor and also engage a reputable, qualified third-party intermediary. To sum all of this up, you will use a 1031 Like-Kind Exchange to avoid paying income taxes or capital gains in the year that you sell the rental property. The exchange rolls (postpones) the tax liability from the property that you sold into the new property that you've bought as long as you follow the rules correctly. Since I have personally seen a failed Like-Kind Exchange, I would encourage you to have your tax advisor, and possibly even your attorney, look over the details of the exchange to ensure that all of the rules are followed. Please see IRS Publication 544 Sales and Other Dispositions of Assets.

Selection of Entity

To LLC or not to LLC, that is the question. My final topic is not whether or not a person should select to do business as yourself or as a business entity. I would leave that to you to consult with your CPA and attorney. I am not licensed to practice law and do not intend to educate you with respect to the legal ramifications of the concept of legal liability. I am going to discuss the different types of entities so that you may speak intelligently with your team.

In my case, I was not required to form an entity to operate my rental operation, but it was encouraged. If I had elected to operate as an individual, I may have put my personal assets at risk. Also, if I chose to operate as a general or limited partnership, the general partner(s) may be subject to risk. I could have chosen to hold my real estate in a corporation, but regular corporations and subchapter S corporations ("C" corporations and "S" corporations) are not advised as entities to hold real estate, as there is a potential problem in liquidating the corporations and creating phantom income. If appreciated property is distributed from a "C" corporation, it can be a deemed sale and dividend, which could create a double tax situation. Similarly, with an "S" corporation, appreciated property distributions can create gains that pass through to the shareholders, creating income but no cash with which to pay the tax. That left me with the most often suggested LLC or limited liability company.

The LLC provides a limited liability exposure to the members, while also providing easy liquidation without tax consequences, or the best of both worlds. An LLC can be set up as a single-member LLC or SMLLC, which is ignored for tax purposes and reported directly on the member's individual income tax return. It can also be set up as a multi-member LLC, which can be treated as a partnership or an "S" corporation for income tax purposes, depending on the desire of the members. Either of these entities passes the income or loss through to the members who are taxed at the individual level. Finally, multi-member LLCs can be either member-managed (all members are managers) or manager-managed (some members are elected as managers). The taxation and liability issues are too numerous to discuss here, so my final recommendation is to consult with your CPA and attorney, especially if you have partners. I chose an LLC because it made sense for me.

In a nutshell

This can be an exciting and fun endeavor. Surround yourself with advisors, determine what your investment goals are, plan ahead, budget and start off on the right foot. It may appear to be a daunting task to begin with, but with the effort comes the reward. In Philippians 3:14, Paul speaks about pressing on toward the mark for the prize. My wife and I both believe that our investment was blessed by God, and he led us to Jeramie to help us achieve our goals. Use the knowledge of others to avoid making the same mistakes everyone else has already made.

Please take what we say to your local firm and let this be a conversation starter with the tax professional who knows you best and understands what you want to do. If you can find one who actually owns and invests in real estate, that's a better move because they can speak from experience. Don't settle for non-action advice from a CPA who is too scared to give you advice on a topic they have no experience in.

Chapter Nine

Eight Ways to Expand Your Nightly Rental Empire - with Brad Moncado

My name is Brad Moncado, and I am a full-time real estate investor. When Jeramie asked me to be a contributor to this book from the perspective of a full-time real estate investor, I leaped at the task to share my knowledge because it didn't come easy. It came with a lot of pain, multitasking, patience, budgeting, strategy and persistence, and the journey has been well worth it. If your goal is to quit your job and replace your income, you can do it. If you are already a full-time investor and want to make better returns on your investment dollars, do not overlook the power of vacation rentals. Once you stop thinking in terms of how many properties you own and start thinking in terms of how many bedrooms you own, you move into an income-driven game with great rewards. I didn't start with vacation rentals; I actually stumbled onto them at one of Jeramie's seminars, and it changed the entire direction of my real estate investment game. The following are eight ways I have discovered that will take your real estate investment goals to the next level.

Believe

It has been my desire for a long time to be a full-time real estate investor. When I was in the corporate world, I was a marketing manager. I always taught my team that "every moment is an opportunity." We worked in an industry where we met new people constantly and offered our product right there on the spot and got an instant commitment from them. If anyone on my team let one moment, one opportunity with a customer slip by, they would never get it back, and that could have been their opportunity to build a relationship and to make a sale. Customers have limitless ways they can spend their time, so making this kind of sale was hard-earned money. "Every moment is an opportunity" was more than a saying, it was my truth. I kept this fact fresh in my mind every day as I worked toward the commitment I made to myself to being a full-time real estate investor.

God works in mysterious ways, and in my business, He is in control. When I did step out as a full-time investor, it was a family decision that we made together and with a great deal of faith. Others around me could see my family's drive and belief, and soon wonderful things started to happen. People began to work with me in ways that I truly can't explain. Out of the blue, friends of mine started sending me various wholesale opportunities, flips, money partners, foreclosures, banker friends, and excellent connections, including Jeramie and his team. Belief was a key factor for me because without the faith to step out and do what I knew I was capable of, I would still be in my corporate job and not living the life I dreamed of.

Before I met Jeramie and discovered nightly rentals, I started an education company with partners, consulted for others in our investor group and began to create my plan for short and long-term success. I decided that doing wholesales and flips were great short-term money. They were a way to keep the lights burning, but starting over with each flip was kind of like having a job. I realized that my long-term financial goals needed some massive restructuring. I started looking for apartments, lease options, storage units, mobile home parks, small lake front resorts, anything that would fit a great buy and hold strategy. I did analysis, crunched the numbers and looked at every opportunity that came to me. Buy and hold seemed to be the best long-term strategy for building long-term wealth. The problem is, I really didn't want to have tenants I had to chase, I didn't really want to have employees and I didn't really want to have to depend on a flip or a wholesale deal to survive. So, I started finding out more about nightly vacation rental from Jeramie. I truly believe that because I wanted a better way to expand my real estate business and because I stayed diligent and faithful in my goals, I found the answers.

Find a good system

The more I crunched the numbers of nightly rentals versus long-term rentals, the better the picture got. Jeramie and his team started coming to our local Real Estate Investor Group (REInvestorGroup.com) and kept talking about vacation rentals. I lived in a resort area and know about the vacation business, but I didn't realize how much money I was leaving on the table by not being involved in it. We talked about the rates of return on one-bedroom condos versus seven-bedroom homes, and a system began to emerge in my brain: regardless of where you live, there is an underserved market. In mine, it was the four to six-bedroom market, so this was the system I began to implement. I looked for any property that would fit this description. Since I had experience remodeling distressed properties, I looked at everything, no matter what shape it was in. My prevailing thought was, if I could get four to six bedrooms in there and have few good amenities, I'd buy it. This made sense to me. A twelve-unit resort with twelve one-bedroom cabins might pull a good return, but you have twelve roofs, twelve air conditioners, and a lot of little cleanings. When I decided exactly what business I wanted to be in, my business started to grow.

Start close to home

The best way to grow an empire is to start in your own back yard. If you do not live in or near a resort area, then look for short-term rentals near a college or stadium. If that doesn't work, then start looking at the nearest vacation destination within an easy drive. Another great option is to buy a property in the city where you love to vacation the most. Your knowledge and passion of the area will fuel your drive. Once you get your first property, you will be looking for another within a year, and it's just as easy to manage one as it to manage two once you get all of your management systems in place.

Connect with the world

When I began to market the property, I did not discriminate on advertising. I listed my home on every by-owner website out there, and what I discovered was that each region of the country has its own vibe. When I would personally look for vacation rentals for my family, I had better success using AirBnB.com when needing a loft in a big city by the ballpark and concert venue.

Other times, HomeAway.com was the most useful to find a home by the beach or in a big city. Stick with what works in your area. Try as many as you feel the most comfortable with, and stick with what is giving you the best result. Don't be afraid to try new ways to learn about this business. When it comes to growth and expansion, you have to go outside of your comfort zone for fresh ideas.

I can't tell you how many tips I've gotten from reading people's blogs, websites, books and from attending seminars. Go connect! Get involved with other vacation rental owners and trade nights. Try this: go on some wonderful vacations with no lodging cost because you've got a property to trade. Once you get to these vacation areas, look into the real estate there, talk to the friends you make in these areas and find out if investing in those new areas are lucrative.

When I first got started investing in real estate, I tirelessly sought out real estate investment clubs to join and get connected to other like-minded people. I soon realized that all of the groups in my area had dried up. So, a friend of mine who was also a real estate investor and I decided to start our own real estate investor group. We ran an ad on Craigslist, met at a local restaurant, and boom, my Real Estate Investor Group was born. I secured REInvestorGroup.com, threw up a website that cost almost nothing, and over the past five years, we have connected to over 400 people locally, as well as large and small real estate investor groups all over the country.

Connecting to a local real estate investor group is a great way to find deals on properties and build a power team around you to help you with your business. You'll have more time to explore more deals and spend less time on the hunt trying to find them by making these great connections.

The power of private equity and owner finance

Once you get started in the nightly rental industry, the real challenge is having enough money to buy all of the properties you want. Banks can get you only so far, and eventually you'll need to tap into the power of private money. Private money, simply put, is money that comes from a group or individual who is tired of the rate of return they are getting on an institutional investment. They will give you the money in the hopes of a better return on their capital. Usually that capital is secured by the real estate you buy, so if you default, the property pays the investor back. There are many private equity groups popping up all over the country, and each one has its own terms. You're best to find an individual to work with, and when you start making that person some money, it won't be long until all of their friends show up and want to do business with you.

How do you find money? Do what most people will not do, and tell them about your business and how it benefits people. As a real estate investor, my twenty-second commercial goes something like this, "I help people get out of properties that need out quick, I help people get into properties that can't normally get into one and I give higher rates of return to people that are not satisfied with what they get now." My commercial for my business gets people's attention. Make a commercial for yourself that gets people's attention, but most importantly, one that is truthful and that you know you can fulfill with your future partners.

One time I was at my son's school band concert, and

I was talking to my father-in-law about the previous year my business and the real estate opportunities I felt that I had missed. As I shared examples of a couple of those missed opportunities, I asked him, "Do you have any money to partner in some investment opportunities?" Before he could answer, the man sitting on the other side of him at the concert, who had listened in to my conversation with my father-in-law, swung his head around and asked me, "How much do you need?" The greatest thing about that story is that when you share your goals, plans and opportunities with people, you never know who is listening. Remember "every moment is an opportunity." In that moment, that gentlemen and I made a connection, and since then, we have partnered on deals that make us both money! That is just one story of how I have found investor money partners. My challenge to you is to create your own real-life example of how you found money partners. I've bought almost every nightly rental I own using private equity, so be brave and have meaningful conversations. Don't let moments pass you by, and most importantly, take care of your private money partners. Doing that will give you the power to grow your business!

Exponential growth in bookings

The more properties you own in one city, the more potential you have for exponential increase in your number of nights booked per property per year. When you advertise one property, you get an average number of calls and emails per month. When you take those calls and emails, you only have one place to put them. Think about it: you spend time and money fielding that inquiry, and if there is something about your property that they don't go for, you've got another property waiting in the wings to tell them about. You are now generating bookings for another property instantaneously, and now each inquiry that comes in is not just an inquiry for one property, but they become an inquiry for your entire group of properties. Keep those emails, keep those contacts and if you have a slow month, use a family member that is internet savvy to blast out some last-minute deals on a property to get it booked. Use a program like constant contact or some web-based vacation rental software to keep track of your past guests. Those are your customers! Stay in touch with them regularly.

The best part about multiple properties is being able to move a guest to another property if an air conditioner goes out or something along those lines. It is sometimes easier to keep your problem solving in-house rather than having to refer them to another owner and potentially pay any increase in rate per night.

Manage properties for other people

Once you are good at this, you can open up more streams of income for yourself (or your family) by managing properties for other people. Your systems and marketing are already in place, so why not add another property and take a percentage? You didn't take on any investment risk, you didn't have to find financing, but you can still earn. Furthermore, you can put the exponential growth practices in place, and it didn't cost you anything to do it. What percentage to charge will depend on the services you provide and your market. It could be anywhere from fifteen to fifty percent, so decide how you can benefit people the most, and get to work.

Love your business and love your people

Maybe I should just sum it up for you: I love this business of having nightly rentals that are vacation homes! My current collection of homes can be found at www.NightlyStay.com. I love to vacation and have stayed in several vacation homes over the years. There is nothing better than having your family all in one home with bedrooms, a kitchen, living areas, a yard, all the things you don't get staying in a hotel. Most of all, it is the memories that are made. I know that my family has created many memories, and I wanted to pay it forward to families when they come to stay in my homes. The financial returns of the business are fantastic, but what's even more rewarding than that is reading the stories that people leave in my guest books.

We all know it is hard to find "investments" that we feel comfortable with, especially in this fear and greed economy. My passion is not only to help families create memories, but also to share my knowledge with potential investors. Love on people every chance you get. People are curious, and you will answer some strange questions when they inquire about your property; it is all part of it. When your passion for your business shows, everyone will notice. Your guests, your friends, your kids, so spread the passion. It is the best way to expand your business. I want this information to be a guide to great returns because I hope that you'll find that, in addition to cash flow and equity, the relationships you make in this industry are worth the price of admission.

Thank You

Thanks for reading Myths, Management & Mastery of Vacation Rentals. Our goal was to shed some light on this industry and to inspire you to take action if this is something you want to do. If you'd like to learn more about vacation rentals and get exclusive, in-depth knowledge of how to locate a top performing vacation rental in any market, you might like to consider looking into:

The Vacation Rental Profit Playbook™

Brad and I have created a great step-by-step help model to help get you started.

Visit us at

VacationRentalProfitPlaybook.com

Made in the USA
San Bernardino, CA
04 February 2016